Wicked COLUMBUS INDIANA

··

PAUL J. HOFFMAN

THE
History
PRESS

Published by The History Press
Charleston, SC
www.historypress.net

Copyright © 2017 by Paul J. Hoffman
All rights reserved

First published 2017

Manufactured in the United States

ISBN 9781625858719

Library of Congress Control Number: 2017931814

Wicked
COLUMBUS
INDIANA

CONTENTS

ACKNOWLEDGEMENTS

I extend my sincere appreciation to the *Republic* newspaper and its owner, AIM Media Indiana, for allowing me access to all of their historical documents. I'd also like to thank Cody Anspaugh, museum assistant at the Bartholomew County Historical Society, and the staff of the Bartholomew County Public Library for help securing photos and information. Thank you to the best copy editor in these parts, Katharine Smith. And finally, I'd like to thank my wife, Kimberly S. Hoffman, for her support and for allowing me to become somewhat of a hermit for several months.

INTRODUCTION

Situated where the Flat Rock and Driftwood Rivers merge to become the East Fork of the White River in south central Indiana, the city of Columbus has a long, proud history.

Known nationwide as one of the smaller cities to boast a vast array of modern architecture, the county seat of Bartholomew County is called home by roughly forty-six thousand residents today. Columbus sits approximately forty miles south of Indianapolis; eighty miles north of Louisville, Kentucky; and ninety miles west of Cincinnati, Ohio.

The high number of notable public buildings and public art in the Columbus area, designed by such well-known and respected individuals as Eero Saarinen, I.M. Pei, Robert Venturi, César Pelli, Harry Weese and Richard Meier, have led to Columbus earning the nickname "Athens of the Prairie."

Two hundred years ago, however, this area was definitely no prairie; it was teeming with lush, green forests, swamps and Delaware Indians.

In its infancy, the locale wasn't even called Columbus. It was called Tiptona after General John Tipton, a famed Indian fighter and prominent landowner who was one of two men to donate thirty acres for the fledgling town; pioneer Luke Bonesteel was the other. Five weeks after being platted, however, the name of the town was changed to Columbus.

Nobody seems to know for sure why Tiptona was scrapped for Columbus. Historians have speculated that Tipton, a Democrat, had an argument with local Whigs, although evidence of that is scarce. It is possible that the new name was used so that pioneers concerned about poor health would

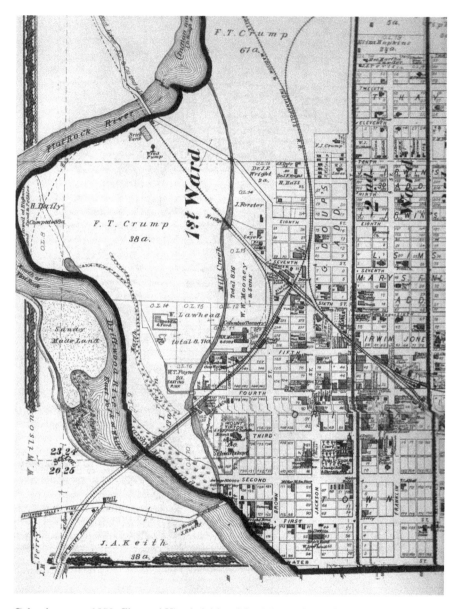

Columbus map, 1879. *Illustrated Historical Atlas of Bartholomew County, Indiana.*

associate this community with the hardy explorer of the New World and/or the well-established Columbus, Ohio.

In 1816, Indiana advanced from a territory to a state, the nineteenth to join the union. Three years later, Bartholomew County was carved out

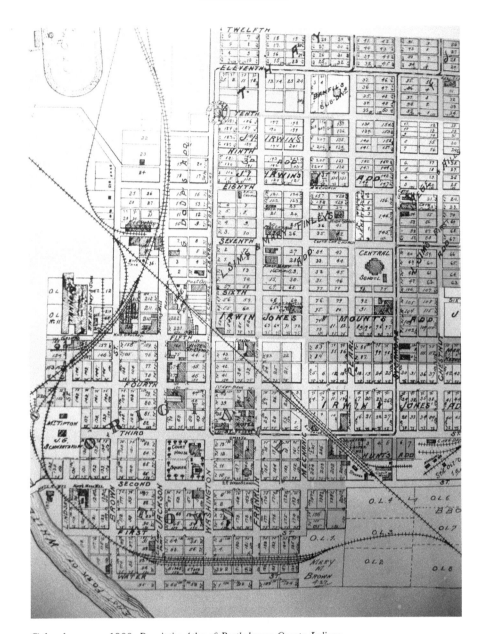

Columbus map, 1900. *Descriptive Atlas of Bartholomew County, Indiana.*

of part of the original Delaware County. Columbus was platted in 1821, becoming the seat of county government immediately. It was incorporated as a town in 1837 and as a city in 1864; residents elected Smith Jones as their first mayor.

Prosperity came to town with the introduction of the railroads in 1844, when the line being laid from Madison to Indianapolis made it to Columbus. That line was followed by connecting routes to the Indiana cities of Jeffersonville, Shelbyville, Hope and Greensburg, as well as to St. Louis and Chicago.

Business boomed during the Civil War, as a local bakery supplied the Union army. Banks were established, which brought stability. Between 1850 and 1900, Columbus's population increased seven-fold, rising from just over one thousand to more than eight thousand.

World War II brought another surge of prosperity, as small, home-owned businesses fulfilled government contracts, and manufacturers such as Cummins, Arvin Industries and Hamilton Cosco all grew during this era. The number of Columbus residents nearly doubled between 1940 and 1960, from 11,738 to 20,778. And the population has more than doubled since then.

Throughout its history, Columbus has maintained a reputation as a safe place to raise a family with a decent standard of living, good schools and wholesome entertainment options.

However, all cities (even ones known as the Athens of anywhere) have had their ups and downs, their unsavory citizens and challenging issues—or just their share of plain old bad luck. The tales told in this book should not be construed as a condemnation of the city as it is today in any way, shape or form. All of the events described in this book are more than thirty-five years old, and many of them are more than a century past.

Many other cities across the country have suffered similar, and even more severe, consequences due to their bad times and people. To their credit, the residents and elected officials of Columbus have more often than not found a way to solve their problems.

With that in mind, I hope you enjoy reading about the unsavory, the unlucky, the challenging and the wicked who have added intrigue to Columbus.

Thank you.

1

FEUDING MAYOR, EDITOR ENGAGE IN STREET FIGHT

*A*mong their duties, reporters and editors are tasked to hold public officials accountable for their statements and actions. And the government is not allowed to infringe on the freedom of the press, a right set out explicitly by the First Amendment to the U.S. Constitution.

When both sides of this equation do their jobs properly, government officials and members of the media form a sort of mutual dependence society. Officials need the newspapers, television and radio stations to disseminate information to their constituents. The media need those officials to provide all the information necessary to tell the public what it needs to know.

When either media members or those appointed or elected to run a particular governing agency fail to do their jobs properly, this system can sputter and perhaps break down, as the parties lose trust or respect for each other. Rarely, though, does the relationship turn so ugly that a government official and a journalist end up in a knock-down, drag-out fistfight.

Columbus saw one of those rare battles on a cold December day in 1877, when the youngest mayor in Indiana and the oldest newspaper editor in the state engaged in quite a battle on a city street.

Looking at biographies of the two combatants today, it might be difficult to understand how two well-respected gentlemen could have ended up in a tussle that left one of them with two black eyes and the other missing some of his whiskers and part of a finger. Mayor George W. Cooper of Columbus

Above: Isaac M. Brown with his
wife, Mary Francis Eddy
Brown, in 1891. *Courtesy
of the* Republic.

Left: George W.
Cooper, 1879.
*Illustrated
Historical Atlas
of Bartholomew
County, Indiana.*

and Isaac M. Brown, editor of the *Daily Evening Republican* newspaper, had stellar reputations, both in their chosen career fields and as people.

The difference was that Cooper made most of his reputation after the fight, while Brown had made his before the altercation. Tensions between the fifty-six-year-old editor and the twenty-six-year-old mayor—ignited by Brown's intense criticism of Cooper's administration and Cooper's distaste for the censure—boiled over into a donnybrook that ended with both men being found guilty of assault and battery and fined.

The paths the men took to their bloodbath were quite different.

In 1821, Brown was born in Centerville, Indiana. He attended Indiana State University and in 1839 went to Paris, Illinois, where he got his start in newspaper work. He made stops at newspapers in Iowa City, Iowa, and Terre Haute, Indiana, where he became one of the founders of the *Daily Terre Haute Express*, the first daily ever published in that city.

In 1862, during the American Civil War, Brown enlisted in the Indiana Cavalry. He was discharged three years later as a first lieutenant. During his service in the Union army, he was captured three times, the first time by his own cousin. After his final capture at Jug Tavern, Georgia, he was placed in prison at Camp Oglethorpe. He was one of six hundred captured officers who were forced to move into an area of Charleston, South Carolina, that was being continually bombarded by the Union in 1864. He was finally exchanged through a special order by Union general William T. Sherman.

Upon his return to Indiana, Brown established the *Sullivan Union* newspaper and served as the Sullivan postmaster. He came to Columbus to help his son Isaac T. Brown run the *Evening Republican*, where he stayed for the rest of his career—a career that earned him posthumous induction into the Indiana Journalism Hall of Fame in 1966.

Upon hearing that Brown had taken over as editor of the *Evening Republican*, newspapers around the state lauded the move. The *Indianapolis Sunday Herald* called Brown a "soldier, editor, printer and gentleman." Brown's previous newspaper, the *Sullivan Union*, had some of the highest praise for him: "The Republicans of Bartholomew County may take it as a compliment in having one of the oldest editors of the state take charge of their county organ. We predict that he will make it hot for Democracy in that county. The experience that Mr. Brown brings to *The Republican* will make it in the future, as in the past, a live paper."

George William Cooper, meanwhile, had not yet built up a lengthy personal history of valor and integrity when he became mayor of Columbus in 1877. Born near Columbus in 1851, he and his family moved into the city

Isaac M. Brown was a Civil War veteran who was captured three times by the
Confederate army. *Courtesy of the* Republic.

when he was eight years old. Cooper graduated from Indiana University at Bloomington in 1872, specializing in academics and law. He was admitted to the bar and commenced practice in Columbus, becoming prosecuting attorney of the city shortly thereafter.

Most of Cooper's positive reputation was fashioned post-fight. Following his stint as mayor, he served as city attorney for four years, was elected as a Democrat to the Fifty-First, Fifty-Second and Fifty-Third Congresses, was chairman of the Committee on Irrigation of Arid Lands and then resumed practicing law in Columbus. He spent twenty-seven years off and on as an attorney, and by the time his career ended, he was considered one of the finest lawyers in the state.

He even raised a giant in the world of journalism. Kent Cooper, who was seven years old at the time of his father's fight with a newspaper editor, became a world-class newsman who directed the development of the Associated Press news service. The younger Cooper got his start as a reporter for the *Columbus Herald*.

The *Daily Republican* had many good things to say about Cooper when it announced his death twenty-two years after his infamous fight with that paper's editor: "George W. Cooper was an honest and a fearless man, exceedingly ambitious and intensely earnest….He had high ideals and he endeavored to live up to them….Mr. Cooper was a man of sound judgement, keen penetration and just discrimination. He was faithful to his friends and true to his convictions."

"On the whole," the editorial continued, "he likely had as few enemies as any other professional man or politician who, of necessity, must always be arrayed against the other man or the other party."

While the paper did note that Cooper could be a little bitter toward his enemies, he would give and take.

When he was younger, though, it seemed that at times, Cooper's take outweighed his give.

About four years prior to the fight, at the age of twenty-two, Cooper allegedly asked a friend to try to pay off someone to vote for him as prosecuting attorney. During the Democratic convention of September 1873, delegate John Denison stood up, held a ten-dollar bill over his head and proclaimed that a friend of Cooper's had given it to him so that he would cast his vote for Cooper. Denison, however, voted for Cooper's foe, Amos Burns, who won the nomination by a mere three votes. Cooper denied ever having seen Denison and also denied authorizing anyone to pay off delegates on his behalf.

A week later, Michael D. Emig, who had filed to run in the race with Cooper and Burns but withdrew before the vote, alleged that Cooper had come to his office before the convention and offered to pay Emig's campaign expenses should Emig drop out of the race. Emig said he refused Cooper's offer and that Cooper returned later in the day and offered $250 if Emig would choose four delegates from Columbus Township who would vote for Cooper if Emig withdrew. Cooper denied this, too, but did later publicly acknowledge attempting to solicit a vote, although he didn't make it clear to which incident he was referring.

By the beginning of 1877, Cooper had become prosecuting attorney and had his sights set higher. In fact, both Brown and Cooper sought the same position that year: mayor of Columbus.

Cooper won the Democratic nomination in the April primary. Brown finished second in both ballots for the Republican nomination. The *Republican* stated that Brown felt he would have won his party's nomination had all his backers shown up at the convention before the balloting began, and the main reason he ran was due to many people telling him that he would make a good mayor.

The general election was held on May 1, with Cooper trouncing the Republican candidate, John Harris, 541 votes to 314. In fact, the Democrats overall routed the Republicans in the city election by an unprecedented margin that year. Cooper, and the rest of the newly elected officials, took office a week later.

The editor was not pleased with the Democratic landslide and made sure his readers knew it. It also didn't take long for the newly elected head of Columbus government and the much-more-senior newspaper editor to start publicly squabbling, only a portion of which can be traced to their political affiliations.

But it seemed there was much more to it than that. An October 18, 1877 story in the *Republican* blasted Cooper for making "bitter and senseless epithets," while in the same story lauding some of the other Democratic speakers when local Dems got together at the county courthouse to celebrate the results of some Ohio elections.

Shortly thereafter, the weekly *Republican* became the *Daily Evening Republican*, which was published each day except Sunday, becoming the first true daily newspaper in town. The newspaper continues today as the *Republic* and was owned by the Brown family from its inception until 2015, with the exception of four years during the 1890s.

It is true that Brown "made it hot" for his enemies, as even his own newspaper would admit years later. "The colonel made it hot alright," the

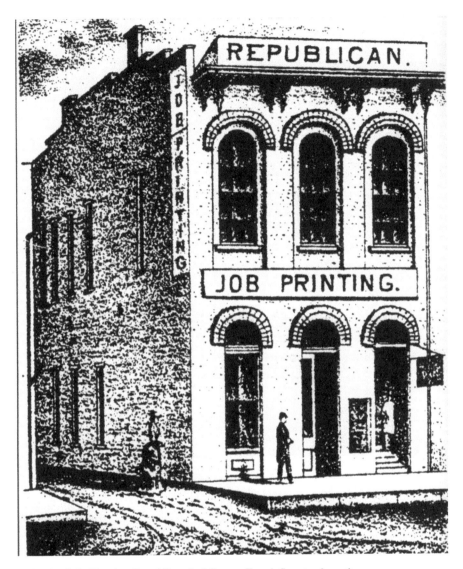

A sketch of the Evening Republican building on Fourth Street, where the newspaper company was located from 1876 to 1882. *Bartholomew County Historical Society.*

paper said in a 1952 special edition celebrating the paper's seventy-fifth year. "When he couldn't pick a verbal fight with Democrat officials in Columbus he started wars with newspapers in neighboring towns."

The final straws that led to the fight were ignited by *Daily Evening Republican* attacks, as Cooper termed them, on public officials. The newspaper laid out several complaints against city government in its November 26 issue. Among the charges levied were:

- The gas company had been digging holes in the city streets to lay pipes but didn't replace the dirt in the proper manner, which made the streets unsafe.
- Hogs roamed the streets free, rooting up sidewalks and yards.
- Cattle were allowed to do the same.
- The streets were not kept clean, and the city ignored the sanitation department's reports.
- Residents placed piles of ashes, and other filth, in the gutters of the streets and were not cited by the city marshal.
- Few arrests were made where the city could not make money in the process.
- The city was full of tramps and vagrants, yet none had been arrested.
- Trains were allowed to block streets for ten to thirty-five minutes despite a state law that any blockage longer than five minutes should incur a fine for every five minutes of obstruction. "Reason, we presume, our city and other officers have a pass to Seymour and Edinburg."
- "A gambling hell is kept in full blast, and Madame rumor says our officials know all about it and are frequent visitors."

Brown wrote that it was unfortunate he had to keep harping on how poor a job the city government had been doing. But he felt compelled, because "when a people is [*sic*] ridden to death by taxation without remuneration no paper is worthy of support unless it assumes the cause of the tax payer, and as a journalist we have the right to speak of these matters as they exist." The editor also said that when officials were in office, they should be scrutinized the same, no matter their political party.

Brown leveled some of his biggest complaints directly at the mayor. He stated that Cooper had made little effort to enforce city ordinances, telling citizens who complain about laws being broken to go into his office and sign an affidavit. Brown questioned this, wondering why the laws were not enforced until a citizen filed an affidavit. Brown answered his own question: "It is done for no other reason than that the responsibility may be shifted upon the shoulders of others."

The editor further lambasted city officials, saying that the law required officials to arrest those who break the laws and that "to stand back and wait or require a citizen to do so is cowardly and shameful."

Finally, Brown suggested that the city officials either do their jobs properly or resign. And if they refuse to resign, "responsible Democrats and Republicans stand ready to hold a public meeting to ask you to do so."

Two days later, on the day before Thanksgiving, the *Daily Evening Republican* asserted that Cooper had suggested "for the credit of the city abroad" that complaints about city government be kept out of the newspapers.

That's when Brown's criticism really escalated.

Isaac M. Brown unmercifully pelted the mayor in his news columns, asking how a mayor can be a credit to his city if, when elected, he could not promise to enforce all the city ordinances. Brown also said that no upstanding man could possibly support Cooper, and he called the mayor's supporters wire-workers, an obsolete term meaning people who secretly control political puppets.

Brown said that Cooper must be giving favors to these wire-workers and intimated more favors were sure to come. It was said that many respected citizens had made such allegations against the city well before those allegations appeared in print. And since these comments most assuredly had made it out into the rest of the state, it was the newspaper's duty to report the facts.

"Had we seen any effort to govern our city as her honor and credit required, and as the tax payers had a right to expect, it is not likely that we should have ever referred to the city government in as plain terms as we have," Brown asserted. He ended his column by calling the city government a mockery.

A couple times throughout this period, Brown also referred to Cooper's involvement in attempting to buy votes prior to the election and implied that the mayor was "a friend of the Whisky ring and the Tammany ring," alleging he supported the business of illegal liquor and he and his cronies were unprincipled officials who enriched themselves by plundering the people.

It was pretty heavy-hitting commentary. It's no wonder Cooper and his fellow government officials got upset. The mayor's reaction, however, went beyond what many considered appropriate.

On Saturday morning, December 1, the day before the fight, Brown was called into the mayor's office and fined two dollars for intoxication. Saloonkeeper Clark Pfeiffer had filed an affidavit against Brown, claiming he had seen him out on the city streets drunk in early November. But Brown said he was home and sober when the incident allegedly occurred.

After getting fined, though, Brown was summoned before Judge Charles Clark and pronounced not guilty "without a moment's hesitation," the *Daily Evening Republican*'s report stated. The newspaper alleged that Pfeiffer had acted at Cooper's urging and the fine was the mayor's way of seeking vengeance for the newspaper's recent commentaries on city government. Clark called the incident "a farce from beginning to end."

The tiff between Cooper and Brown finally escalated into a public physical confrontation on Sunday, December 2. It was alleged in reports in the *Evening Republican* that the mayor stood on a street corner in front of D.W. Adams drugstore, at 315 Washington Street in the Odd Fellows building, for two hours waiting for Brown with the intention of provoking a fight. Cooper was also accused of making sure the police and city marshal were kept away from the site.

The city's Democratic newspaper, the *Bartholomew Democrat*, however, alleged that Brown had expressed the belief that he could whip the mayor, indicating the newspaperman was the one who was looking for a fight.

Witnesses interviewed by the *Republican* said that Cooper had told someone he was "looking for old man Brown and was going to give him hell" and that on the day of the fight, Cooper "looked like he wanted to attack Brown." Another witness allegedly said that he had seen the mayor talking with a policeman shortly before the mêlée and felt that something just was not right about the situation.

Brown left his office on the north side of Fourth Street between Washington and Franklin and headed north on Washington Street. When Brown walked Cooper's way, the mayor was standing with several other men. Brown said that as soon as he made his way to where the men were standing, Cooper unleashed a long string of insults at him. Brown said he held his tongue as long as he could, but when Cooper said that were Brown not an old man, he would whip the hell out of him, Brown responded.

He put his hand on Cooper's chest and said that the mayor of Columbus ought to be ashamed to have made such a remark. Cooper continued blasting Brown with insulting language, Brown said, until a fight finally commenced, with Cooper throwing the first punch.

Brown complained that the mayor didn't give him time to remove his King William–style overcoat before the physical attack, leaving him at a decided disadvantage—as if their thirty-year age difference and a decided weight advantage in Cooper's favor wasn't enough already.

Cooper's punch sent Brown reeling backward off the curb and onto the street, whereupon Cooper jumped on him and hit him again. The skirmish

Washington Street looking north from Third Street. Mayor George Cooper and Isaac M. Brown, editor of the *Evening Republican*, fought on the right side of the street just past the wagon pictured. *Bartholomew County Historical Society.*

left Brown with a pair of black eyes, and Cooper lost some whiskers and part of a thumb or finger to Brown's gnawing and scratching. The fight was ended when James Godfrey broke things up.

The immediate aftermath of the fight was nasty, too.

Brown's newspaper the next day lambasted the mayor. His son Isaac T. Brown signed his name to the following note in the left-hand column near the top of the first page: "I want the Mayor of Columbus, and all others interested, to know that I hold myself responsible for what appears in these columns, and any redress demanded should be made to me."

The younger Brown sought Cooper's resignation:

> *A more dastardly and premeditated attack never was made upon an editor or citizen, by any city official, and we shall now favor a public meeting of all parties to be held at the courthouse as soon as possible to publicly demand the resignation of the Mayor as an unworthy official....*
>
> *If we had a yellow dog that was guilty of so contemptible an act, we should take him out and shoot him. Truly, the Mayor isn't fit company for a cur* [mongrel].

That edition of the paper also rehashed virtually every complaint the newspaper had made against Cooper and the current city administration since the election, adding in a few more allegations, insinuations and rumors that had not been previously printed. It was written that Cooper was a friend of the green blind (drinking establishments that did not follow the liquor laws) and had engaged in playing cards in one of the illegal "gambling hells" in town within the past two weeks. The publisher finished this particular diatribe with this admonishment: "Let the people blush for the Mayor since all shame has long since forsaken him."

But Isaac T. Brown didn't stop there. He threw a few more choice words at Cooper on his pages, calling the mayor "a pitiful coward," "this thing, this mass of flesh thrown together in rude shape and topped out with bristles that stand on end like quills upon the fretful porcupine," a "corrupt sneak" and finally, yes, "a nincompoop."

Reaction to the fight was decidedly in the newspaperman's favor, at least according to reports in the *Republican*. The city treasurer, William Abbot, resigned his position immediately, with the *Republican* insinuating that the move was due to Cooper's attack on Isaac M. Brown.

Many other newspapers defended Brown.

The *Madison Evening Star* called Brown a "game old editor" who was "making a brave fight for the honor and fair fame of the beautiful little city of Columbus." It said that the *Republican* was doing its best to fight gambling, illicit liquor sellers and prostitution, but Brown was meeting resistance from "mean and unfair opposition from the very people who were supposed to assist him in this venture."

The *Madison Courier* said that the *Evening Republican* columns "glow and burn with righteous heat in behalf of the citizens of Columbus and against an inefficient and crime-permitting city government."

The *Edinburgh Courier* also praised Brown's journalistic efforts. "That *The Republican* has tread upon the most tender corn of Mayor Cooper is nothing more than its duty if he knowingly permits and winks at violations of the law."

The *Indianapolis Journal* thought that Brown's "fearless exposure of the mayor" should have served as a wake-up call for Cooper. Instead, it only made him angry, and Cooper then disgraced his office.

The *Greencastle Banner* said: "It is disgraceful that he [Brown] should be beaten for having done his duty to the public as a journalist....Columbus needs a new mayor. No wonder the town has a poor reputation as of late."

The *Hope Independent* went so far as to call Cooper "a notorious coward."

Not all newspapers were completely supportive of Brown, though.

The *Shelbyville Volunteer* chided Brown for publishing stories critical of local government: "You are a very ancient editor, but it is evident your lengthy career has not taught you that discretion...is the better part of valor. We told you as soon as you opened your mouth on politics, you would put your foot in it." The *Volunteer* did sympathize with Brown but thought the editor would have learned by now that "the tiger always beats everybody who plays against him."

The *Sullivan Democrat*, while stating that it thought the fight was all Cooper's doing, felt that the *Republican* maybe complained about city officials more vociferously than was healthy.

The *Bartholomew Democrat*—as was to be expected—came down heavily against Brown. The *North Vernon Sun* complained that the *Republican* had failed to print notices it had received that were unfavorable toward its editor. It seems a previous snit between the *Sun* and *Republican* editors might have helped provoke those negative comments, though.

In the days following the fight, the *Evening Republican*'s pages continued complaining about the mayor and his administration. The most interesting story on the alleged evils of the local government was what the paper said was a link between the mayor and a gambling house that was supposedly operating in the building next door to Cooper's office.

In its coverage, the *Republican* included a diagram of the supposed gambling house and the mayor's office. Cooper's desk and windows, shown facing Tipton Street (now Third Street), were marked with letters. Also shown was a wall between the mayor's office and gambling rooms, both of which were on the second floors of their respective buildings. The diagram showed the location of a door to a faro bank (French card game) room as well as a card table.

The story said that to access the gambling rooms, one had to either walk up a staircase inside Palmer and Maynard's saloon on the north side of Tipton Street between Washington and Jackson or enter through an alley off Washington Street. It was also estimated that the mayor's desk was a mere eighteen feet from the card table.

The description of the place was provided to the *Evening Republican*, the newspaper reported, suggesting that "officers preserve it for future reference if it should so happen they would ever have use for it, which is extremely doubtful under the current administration."

The paper also printed state laws spelling out the duties of mayors and other city officials, along with the statements the current Columbus mayor and marshal were said to have made promising to uphold the law when they were sworn in. The conclusion the *Republican* expected readers to come to was that neither Cooper nor city marshal Ben F. Fewell had lived up to what they had promised to do or to what the law stated they should.

The *Bartholomew Democrat* backed the Democratic mayor throughout this whole sequence of events, although apparently not nearly as strongly as the *Republican* hounded him. The *Democrat* did attack the *Evening Republican*, though, as "an enemy to the city of Columbus, and has on many occasions intemperately opposed its best interests."

The *Democrat* also questioned whether Brown's motive in attacking Cooper was really to gain the mayor's office for himself. Brown retorted that he had no such aspirations, but that if the job were offered and he accepted that he figured "the best way to reform Columbus would not be fighting in the streets."

The *Democrat* also alleged that one of its reporters went into Palmer and Maynard's but could find no evidence of gambling rooms. So it couldn't understand why the *Republican* asserted there was indeed such a place on the premises.

Both Cooper and Brown were charged with assault and battery and went to trial. Both were found guilty and fined $1 plus court costs, totaling $70 (worth about $1,500 today). Cooper maintained his innocence and threatened not to pay his fine. He eventually did, but not until after Judge George W. Arnold made out a court order that Cooper be taken to jail if he didn't pay it.

The court's decision seemed to have a positive effect on all parties involved.

The *Evening Republican* praised the news that the mayor had been found guilty: "In this decision, his honor maintains the freedom of the press and the rights of the people to inquire into and criticize the actions of the officers."

Meanwhile, the paper's personal attacks of the mayor and other city officials virtually ended, and its complaints against them decreased in number and tone. More stories started appearing that praised city officials when they did uphold the law.

This is not to say that the *Republican* didn't offer its opinion when city government failed to act as the newspaper thought it should. Wishes that the marshal would raid the gambling house next door to the mayor's office continued to be made. But the tone of these offerings was less sharp than before the fight.

Isaac M. Brown retired about six months after the fight. He died at his home at 528 California Street on December 1, 1891, at the age of seventy after a two-month illness. The announcement of his death in the *Evening Republican* said he was a man of great courage and strong mind; he was slow to form an opinion, but that once he had an opinion he was slow to give it up; he was kind-hearted and sympathized with the distressed; he was very emotional and quick to tears; and those who knew him would remember him for his manhood.

Cooper, meanwhile, went on to a distinguished political and legal career. He died in Chicago on November 27, 1899, at the age of forty-eight after three years of being incapacitated. He went through many physical ailments in his later years and had a finger amputated in 1898. A year later, he had a rib removed. He also had an operation performed due to tuberculosis of the knee.

Their physical fracas didn't sully their reputations for good, and it probably led to better teamwork between the media and city government here, albeit with a nudging from a judge.

As the *Lawrenceburg Register* noted at the end of 1877: "It is said to be perfectly quiet in Columbus at present—the peace and dignity of the State having been fully vindicated."

2

The Other Side of the Tracks

$\mathscr{A}$s with most cities, Columbus has had its share of downtrodden neighborhoods over the years. For most of its history, the areas that housed the poorest residents and were plagued by higher crime rates than other parts of the city were situated along the west and south sides of Columbus.

Smoky Row, Jug Row, Happy Hollow and Death Valley all pretty much fell into this pattern of substandard housing and higher crime rates.

Smoky Row was perhaps the first area of the city that parents warned their children about and that respectable folk avoided. It was situated along the west end of First Street on the far south side of the city. One of Columbus's first red light districts intermingled with rough houses, both in appearance and in clientele, on Smoky Row.

The term "Smoky Row" has been used to describe many poor neighborhoods in various cities over the years and occasionally appears as a generic term for such an area. By the mid-1870s, Columbus's version was already well known for disturbances, prostitution and other assorted crimes.

The Row's reputation was alluded to, albeit in a somewhat sarcastic manner, in a December 10, 1877 report in the *Evening Republican*: "The peace and quiet of Smoky Row was again disturbed this morning. Two irate females engaged in a little quarrel, and but for the timely arrival of friends would have undoubtedly snatched each other bald-headed. We were beaten out of a first-class local, and the denizens of that part of the city an exciting sensation."

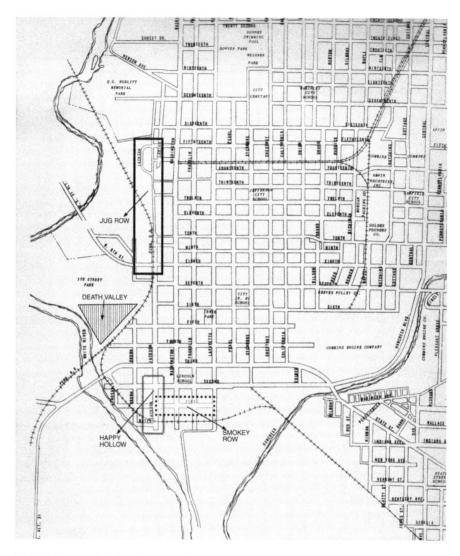

This 1963 map of Columbus shows the approximate locations of some of the city's worst slum areas. *Courtesy of the* Republic.

Later in the month, the newspaper lamented the dismal state that Smoky Row had become, announcing that "now there is a regular John Allen dance house on Smoky Row. Admission is 25 cents to all parts of the house. Dances held on Tuesdays." There was often much more than dancing going on at these soirees. What the notice was saying was that there was now a house of prostitution on the Row. John Allen was a notorious dance hall owner and pimp who ran places all over New York City in the 1850s and '60s.

In the years that followed this pronouncement, the dances became more regular on the Row.

A dance that involved girls as young as twelve years old was broken up by police in December 1884. It was held at a private house on Sycamore Street, but the "roughs" and the young girls had been collected from Smoky Row and other disreputable parts of Columbus.

The incident sparked the *Republican* to plead for stiffer sentences for such crimes in its December 24, 1884 edition. "Just so long as fines are one cent and [court] costs $12.70, just so long will houses of ill fame flourish and be filled with lewd women, just so long will our citizens be annoyed by thieves."

Fights were common in Smoky Row.

One of the better stories of a Smoky Row fight was the one reported of a July 1882 engagement between Mike Fisher and Paul Sheets. It started with the two insulting one another. Then the fists came out, resulting in "a first-class pugilistic contest." Sheets was said to have had the better of the action during "the mauling part of the performance" and "used his antagonist rather roughly, in fact, simply beat the stuffin' out of him," the *Republican* reported.

It wasn't just the men who got into fights on Smoky Row. Women got into the action, too. Perhaps Mike Fisher's wife learned some roughhousing techniques from her husband, as she was arrested a few years after Mike's famous fight for a dust-up with Maggie Burrell.

One woman, a so-called "soiled dove" from Brown County, came to Smoky Row in June 1884 and created quite a ruckus. Jane Wilson went calling on a former acquaintance of hers, a Mr. Lacy of the Row. Mr. Lacy was not inclined to renew this relationship and told Jane to leave. Jane did not appreciate being rebuffed and attacked his door "with the fury of a cyclone" and vowed that she would get in. Her screams attracted a great crowd. Police came but needed help to subdue the woman. She kicked a man named Lame Charley away from her before four men took hold of one limb apiece and carted her off to jail.

Most of the fights ended up with black eyes, bruised flesh, fines or sometimes short jail stays. Once in a while, the violence turned into something worse.

Smoky Row's William Smith was charged with shooting his estranged wife and brother in January 1885. He was acquitted, but such violent outbursts were becoming the norm in the Row. The violence in the area started to get so bad that the *Republican* once warned city residents to anticipate war in Europe and war on Smoky Row.

One time a man came to town from Jennings County, got drunk and made such a nuisance of himself in Smoky Row that even the people who lived in that rat hole were said to be disturbed by his antics.

Besides the violence, the living conditions were deplorable.

One night in July 1879, a Mrs. Mutz, living on Smoky Row, was awakened by a sharp pain on her chest. She reached up and grabbed a rat that was biting her left breast. Blood flowed profusely. "We have often heard of rats eating a dead body," a newspaper report on the incident noted, "but it is seldom that we have to record a case where they attacked and wounded a living person."

Around Christmas 1880, the *Republican* caught wind of a family living in the basement of a Smoky Row house in "a horrible condition of poverty and filth." There was no heat in the room, and the children were crawling around nearly naked. The newspaper pleaded with those who were of a charitable manner to help the family.

Alcohol abuse was rampant on Smoky Row. And the problem sometimes involved children.

"One of the most disgusting sights seen on the streets of our city for some time was that of a boy almost thirteen years old, a denizen of Smoky Row, who was staggering drunk on Washington Street last evening," a story in the January 15, 1880 *Republican* said.

Some of the worst Smoky Row had to offer was on display in 1885. The *Republican*, in a March 7 story titled "Smoky Row: Its Characters, Their Grievances, Their Methods of Revenge," likened the area to its famous namesake in Nashville, Tennessee, saying that Nashville might have more evil in its Smoky Row, but Columbus's version featured citizens who were as bad or worse.

The first sentence of that story said a mouthful:

> *The far famed Smoky Row of Nashville, Tenn., even in the palmiest days of its wretchedness and filth during the [Civil] war, never furnished to the world beings more utterly depraved than does the locality in this city that is known by the above sweet scented name, every letter of which is suggestive, by association, of filth, squalor, lewd women, disease, curses, drunkenness, foul mouthed men capable of the most outrageous crimes, murder if it was necessary to their schemes.*

The condemnation of the local Smoky Row continued:

The mid-night orgies held in some of the so-called houses and cellars of the Row, include draughts from the flowing bowl of the vilest whiskey, demonic dances by the squeaking of an old fiddle, unhallowed embraces between those loathsome with disease, and other things whose mention should not fall on the cultivated ear.

In October 1885, an argument on Smoky Row over a love interest ended in one woman getting shot. It started when two young ladies, Emma Knotts and Mattie Stewart, were both attracted to Ed Moyer. The jealousy erupted one night when Moyer and the Knotts girl were taking a stroll, and the Stewart girl came upon them. After the girls exchanged words, Stewart said that she would shoot Moyer if she had a gun. Moyer at once pulled out a .32-caliber revolver and handed it to Stewart. Instead of carrying out her threat, though, Stewart took off with the revolver. Moyer chased after her to retrieve the weapon.

During the excitement, Martha Greiner came upon the scene. She called Stewart some choice names and slapped the girl on the cheek, which caused Stewart to wave the revolver in front of her face to stave off the blows. In so doing, the gun discharged a bullet that nicked Greiner's ear.

Shortly thereafter, things started quieting down, even if just a tad, on Smoky Row. By the 1920s, the area wasn't even known as Smoky Row anymore, and eventually all the residences were torn down.

Other Columbus neighborhoods had bad reputations over the years. And one street, Jackson, was the location of two of them.

Jug Row occupied the northern part of Jackson Street and Happy Hollow the extreme southern end of the street, across from the Pennsylvania Railroad yards. There was a time in the early 1900s when both areas were plaguing Columbus simultaneously.

Happy Hollow, sometimes referred to as Happy Holler, was prone to flooding from the East Fork of the White River, and living conditions there were substandard.

A cold, windy and snowy start to March 1899 had many city residents low on provisions. It was especially bad in the poorer areas of town, including Happy Hollow, where a newspaper report said "a family of eight was huddled together this morning around a cook stove."

When the White River flooded in January 1904, nearly everyone in Happy Hollow was forced to evacuate. Two families stayed behind, and one man brought food home for dinner via rowboat.

The rain continued, and by late March, the water was as high as it had been in eight years. Happy Hollow was a virtual ghost town. Everyone had either already moved out or were planning to leave. Residents came back after the river receded, and a levee was built along the river from the Second Street Bridge south about a quarter of a mile.

Unfortunately, the levee broke in May of the following year when the river rose again, and the water came within a few feet of houses in the Hollow. Water covered surrounding farm fields to the west and south, and numerous large fish, including buffalo fish weighing up to fifteen pounds, were thrown into the fields by the torrents. Floodwaters returned the following spring, and once again, Happy Hollow residents either left or used boats to get to their neighbors or dry land.

Flooding wasn't the only problem that Happy Hollow faced. The area was well known for intoxicated folks getting into fights or committing vandalism and residents engaging in prostitution.

An example of the rough nature of Happy Hollow arose in June 1901. Police were called to the house of a Mrs. Shatto, who was loudly using profanity. She gave authorities quite a tussle before finally being subdued. Police found brass knuckles under her pillow.

The beginning of the end of Happy Hollow came following some newsworthy crimes involving children.

The first of these was the kidnapping of a fourteen-year-old girl by a middle-age Columbus widower. John Harden took off on foot with Lizzie Elkins, a Happy Hollow resident, on August 18, 1908, about three weeks after Harden was found guilty of assault and battery for pinching a woman so hard he gave her several bruises.

Not long after that, twenty-year-old William "Cat" Heitz was charged with raping a fourteen-year-old girl there. He pleaded guilty to contributing to the girl's delinquency, and the rape charge was dropped.

In early 1909, Happy Hollow's Charles Osborne, an eighteen-year-old man, was found guilty of raping an eleven-year-old girl there and was sent to the Jeffersonville prison.

Around the same time, a fifteen-year-old boy and a twelve-year-old girl were charged with delinquency. The boy wandered the streets and railroad yards day and night, smoked, used vile and vicious language and was incorrigible. The girl didn't have much better manners.

Public outrage demanded that Happy Hollow be cleaned up.

"Some of these boys and girls claim that they do not know any better," read the *Republican* on February 26, 1909. "They have lived in poverty and

MORE CHILDREN CAUGHT IN NET

Revolting Stories of Happy Hollow are to be Told Again.

THREE CHAPTERS NOW

WITHIN PAST FEW MONTHS THREE GIRLS HAVE BEEN ARRESTED ON MOST SERIOUS CHARGES, OLDEST ONE BEING FOURTEEN.

The revelation in 1909 of revolting stories involving children in Happy Hollow signaled the beginning of the end of that area. *Courtesy of the* Republic.

squalor all their lives. Their homes are the meanest sorts of hovels and they learned to swear and blackguard as they learned to talk. Something ought to be done to clean up that end of town and put an end to the youthful tragedies which have been coming to light so rapidly the past few months."

Shortly thereafter, the Central Indiana Lighting Company started work on a new power plant near Happy Hollow on Washington Street between First and Second. By the middle of 1909, the *Republican* was touting how well behaved the citizens had gotten. "Happy Hollow is as peaceful and serene as any of the curb and gutter districts of Columbus," the paper said, crediting the new power plant for garnering folks' attention there.

Just up the street from Happy Hollow, Jug Row's reputation as a place of profanity, houses of ill repute and the like started well before 1900 and lasted into the 1920s. The area's name came from the jugs area residents toted north to the artesian "stink well" at the far north end of Jackson Street at Thirteenth, where they got their water. The jugs were so common that just about everyone in that area had one, and the jugs passed from house to house.

The area was bounded on the north by the stink well; on the east by the mule playground, sometimes referred to as Sanitarium Park, on North Washington Street; on the south at roughly Sixth Street; and on the west by Frank Crump's brickyard and the river.

During its run as a nasty place to be, Jug Row featured Lillian "Todie" Tull's notorious house of ill repute at 910 North Jackson. The Pennsylvania Railroad Depot was at Seventh and Jackson, and the Ceraline Manufacturing Company's new mill was between Seventh and Eighth Streets west of Jackson. Part of that mill still stands and is a portion of the corporate headquarters of Cummins Inc.

Frank Thomas's Cyclone Saloon graced Seventh and Jackson and was the site of one of the area's first major incidents in July 1890. Jay "Jaybird" McDonald walked into the saloon and laid a silver dollar on the bar to pay for a drink. Thomas put several coins on the bar to count out change for McDonald, who was accused of taking a five-dollar piece from among the coins. Thomas confronted McDonald, who denied taking it.

The bartender, Daniel Sine, saw that trouble was brewing, so he stepped between the men. But McDonald got past Sine and rushed at Thomas, wielding a knife. With an upward stroke, McDonald cut off a small piece of the saloon owner's ear and also left a four-inch gash across Thomas's face. A small artery was hit, causing quite a flow of blood, and Thomas was lucky to survive.

McDonald left. He returned thirty minutes later but was refused admittance. He went to the back of the building and summoned Sine. When the bartender showed up, old Jaybird gave him the five-dollar coin he'd stolen. That didn't satisfy anyone, and McDonald was soon arrested and prosecuted.

In July 1909, fifty-three residents of Jug Row were asked to testify in an investigation conducted by prosecutor William V. O'Donnell and Justice W.W. Stader. The testimony reportedly revealed much of the nastiness that Jug Row had to offer.

"The conditions along Jug Row as set forth by some of the witnesses were revolting in the extreme and almost beyond belief that they could exist among civilized people and in a community that made even the slightest pretentions at morality," the *Republican* reported, adding that some people of high rank and respectability were involved. "The wild debauches in which the denizens of that locality have indulged puts anything of that kind in previous years to shame."

The newspaper refused to print some of the most lurid testimony because it was so nasty, it "could not be printed on asbestos paper." The report concluded that the anthem of Jug Row had changed from "There'll be a Hot Time in the Old Town Tonight" to "The Judgement Day Is Coming."

The investigation hit a snag when several witnesses couldn't be located later; some had even moved out of the city. But enough witnesses were willing to spill the beans on illegal activities going on in their neighborhood that by the first week of August, authorities were making loads of arrests. Three husband-and-wife duos were locked up over one weekend, facing a slew of charges, from giving liquor to minors and statutory rape to contributing to the delinquency of children and running a house of prostitution. Most of them faced multiple charges.

Events started to ebb in Jug Row around 1912 or so. After one particular court case that year, prosecutor Ralph Spaugh said that "he would proceed to break up the lawlessness in the neighborhood or fill the county jail full of prisoners in the attempt."

That summer, a new shirt factory opened between Washington and Jackson Streets. The Reliance Manufacturing Company opened with seventy-three employees at 1220 Washington Street. A couple of months later, the factory employed two hundred girls and women. At the same time, the houses on Jug Row that were owned by Francis T. Crump got a new coat of paint and were cleaned up.

JUG ROW NO LONGER SPELLS DISRESPECT

For the Houses and Premises Along the Row Have Undergone a Change for the Better.

There is a block of houses on north Jackson street just south of the Crump "stink well," which for many years has been known as jug row, so named because of the many jugs that are taken to and from the "stink well."

By June 1912, the Jug Row area of north Jackson Street had finally been cleaned up. *Courtesy of the* Republic.

Another area that was literally on the other side of the tracks was a pox on Columbus for the first half of the twentieth century. Death Valley was sandwiched between the White River and the Pennsylvania Railroad tracks at the west end of West Fourth and Fifth Streets. It was plagued by rats, disease, substandard housing and flooding. The poorest of the poor lived here from the depths of the Great Depression until the early 1960s. Even poor people in Columbus's other blighted neighborhoods felt sorry for the people who lived in Death Valley.

Flooding was a constant problem. In January 1937, approximately fifty Death Valley families were rendered homeless by high water, and more than one dozen dogs had to be evacuated from the pound that was then located there. Residents needed help from the Red Cross and other charitable folks to replace possessions ruined by the water. The flooding problems persisted throughout Death Valley's existence.

Crime was also an issue, although living conditions were the biggest problem.

Death Valley had gotten so bad by 1937 that when twenty-four members of the Social Service Association took a tour of the slum that May, the local charitable group reported that the cabins were squalid.

The Social Service Association visited again in October and unanimously adopted a resolution to make better housing in Death Valley an immediate project for the group. It was to be part of a plan to improve living conditions all over Columbus and East Columbus, the largest such operation ever undertaken here.

Death Valley was given first priority. But by December, the group hadn't made any progress, and the city sanitary officer, John Coovert, reported that despite the situation being brought to the attention of the state board of health, no action had happened yet.

The following February, Death Valley and its residents were made a topic of discussion among representatives of the welfare department, health department and city government. The discussion centered on whether it would be better to eradicate the area or to try to improve it. The property was owned by W. Curtis Robertson, who lived at Fourth and Jackson Streets. He told the officials that he was willing to do anything to improve the property.

Mayor John L. Hosea suggested building barracks and separating them into apartments. But he said that even if this were done, it wouldn't be long before those were uninhabitable, too. He also said that there was no other place for the residents to go while any new construction was done.

Unfortunately, little was done, and the misery of Death Valley lived on.

In November 1943, a two-room house at the end of West Fourth Street was destroyed by fire, leaving Mr. and Mrs. Luther Johnson and their five children (all nine years old or younger) homeless. Everything the family had, except for a daybed and a heating stove, was consumed. Among the losses were one hundred pounds of potatoes the father had just purchased after receiving a paycheck from the Pennsylvania Railroad. The family moved into a barn in Death Valley in which another family was already residing.

The rat problem was horrific in Death Valley, and they came out of nearby fields and wooded areas when the floods hit. In April 1939, during another bout of high water, Mel Christopher, in charge of the dog pound, said that

Death Valley, home to hundreds of families from the 1930s to the early 1960s, was often flooded, had sub-standard housing and was infested with rats. *Courtesy of the* Republic.

his brother-in-law, Alex Baker, had killed 140 rats in the neighborhood and that hundreds of others had gotten away.

The city made cleaning up Death Valley its number-one priority in its 1948 master plan. It didn't happen.

One plan to help clean up the area was the installation of a new sewer line in 1952. The sewer was seen as perhaps a means to eradicate the poor conditions there. Any toilets added would have to be connected to the new line. But instead of landlords building homes with toilets connected to the sewer line, there was simply no more new construction in Death Valley, and the population there started to decrease slowly.

In 1953, West Fourth Street was closed off at the railroad tracks, leaving the only entrance and exit to Death Valley at the west end of Fifth Street. The move was made so that the Pennsylvania Railroad could park cars on a siding at that location.

A conversation between two Death Valley residents, after witnessing a fire destroy a barn used as a home and threaten many other overcrowded shanties in 1954, told the attitude of many residents. One resident said, "It might not have been a bad idea if everything had been destroyed. We wouldn't have lost much." But another resident replied, "It's the only place we've got to live because nobody wants to rent [to you] if you've got children."

A reporter and a photographer from the *Republican* went into the neighborhood in May 1957 to document living conditions because, the story said, most residents of Columbus had never set foot "on the other side of the tracks."

Speaking about one family of four, the reporter stated, "I saw a lean-to type of dwelling built with old boards and packing cases right on the river's edge. High waters during flood stage along the river had left its traces of mud and silt over the entire structure. The doorway was open and without a screen, even though the mosquitoes were swarming in droves."

The house was anchored to two-foot-high posts, and high waters had warped the floorboards and left them covered with silt and mud. A flat-topped, drum-shaped, wood-burning stove was the main feature of one of the two rooms of the dwelling. Two tables and an old washing machine sitting lopsided completed the furniture array. On top of a table was a dishpan with dirty dishes piled up. On the other table sat a few groceries and some dish soap. Most of the bedroom was taken up by the bed. A small vegetable garden and a pile of wood sat outside, along with an old upholstered chair sitting by the door and some hens pecking at rolled oats that had been thrown to them. The lady of the house said the family had been trying to save money to buy a lot. If they could do that, they certainly would like to move out.

By September of that year, the *Evening Republican* editor, Robert E. Gordon, suggested that it might be possible for groups around the city to organize to purchase the land in Death Valley and develop a park there. He said that the discussion of "slum clearance" had been on many leaders' lips for some time, but it had gotten to the point where the time for action was now. He acknowledged that the first question was what to do with the residents. He said that educating them on how improving their living conditions would raise their families' fortunes might be part of the solution. But there was more to it than just that.

A mother wrote of her trip to Death Valley when delivering food to the needy during the holidays in 1957, and the letter was published in the *Evening Republican*, no doubt pulling at the heartstrings of many local residents. The woman and a fireman assigned to help her deliver the baskets arrived at a Death Valley home that sported boarded-up windows, a broken door and wood floors. They had to place the food on the floor since there were no cabinets.

The woman said that one little boy, when he saw the food, asked, "Is there any meat?" She assured him there was, which prompted one of the biggest smiles the woman had ever seen. When they left the house in the rain and mud, the woman heard a voice call to her. A little boy with no coat on asked, "Do you have any food for us?" He was joined by a girl with a light sweater.

The woman had to apologize for not having any that day, but if they would tell their parents to contact the police or firemen, they might be able to deliver some. The woman, heartbroken over her encounters in Death Valley, asked readers, "Of course, we are all very busy, but is there anyone who can't find the time to help a child if he were to be asked 'Is there any meat?' or 'Do you have any food for us?'"

She wondered if some long-term solution to the deplorable conditions and extreme poverty could be found. "Wouldn't it be wonderful in the years to come if these little children we met today would not be in the same heart-rendering situation as their parents are today! How much do you care?"

A group of civic-minded people took a tour of some of Columbus's blighted areas in March 1958. The group found Death Valley especially disturbing. The *Evening Republican* columnist Bernard Hunter was among the group and detailed some of the tragedy he witnessed. "The insides of these homes are appalling, unbelievable filth and squalor," he wrote. Hunter described shacks cobbled together from

Two photos of the poor living conditions in Death Valley on May 4, 1957. *Courtesy of the* Republic.

wood scraps, tin, tar paper and cardboard, most of which had dirt floors. Large families oftentimes lived in cramped quarters, and they wore clothes that "we wouldn't consider allowing our pets to sleep on." He said that many people were in that condition due to no fault of their own. And he also lamented the fact that very few people with means were willing to help.

Things wouldn't turn around for a while in Death Valley, though.

Two of the houses in Death Valley were razed in May 1959, leaving eight houses. Rent at the time was between ten and twelve dollars per month.

Finally, a discussion during a public lunch in 1962 led to some real headway on cleaning up Death Valley. Mayor E.A. Welmer met with Bruce Warren of Dunlap and Company; Carl Miske, president of the downtown development association; park director Bill Wilson; and Irwin Union Bank and Trust president S.E. Lauther. The men bandied about the idea that Death Valley could become a park.

A year later, the Mooney Tannery property immediately north of Death Valley was put up for sale, and Warren wondered if the rest of the properties in that area could be acquired and turned into a park.

In May 1963, the mayor brought twenty civic representatives together to discuss a plan whereby the city would purchase nearly sixty-seven acres of land along the east bank of the White River, including the entirety of Death Valley. The mayor figured the cost would be $143,000 to purchase the land between Fourth and Eighth Streets, the river and the railroad tracks, and it could be raised by businesses, organizations and individuals.

A meeting shortly thereafter on May 17 attracted two hundred people to Donner Center, where plans for a new park were made. There was a degree of urgency involved since the Howes Leather Company, which owned the former Mooney Tannery building, gave an option to sell that property for $80,000, but the option ran only until June 1. A total of five tracts of land needed to be purchased from five landowners to create the mayor's vision.

Reaction was swift. By the end of the day, $61,100 was pledged to the project, and a total of $113,000 was raised within just one week of the Donner Park meeting. The goal was increased to $150,000 because so many residents wanted to ensure immediate clearance of the properties involved, the tannery building, the homes in Death Valley and brush, for what was unofficially called Tipton Park. Virtually all of the money needed was raised by June 7, and the properties had been purchased or options exercised.

Death Valley was the first area of the future park to get bulldozed. By the beginning of August, it was no more.

Elwood Allen, a park planner from Bennington, Vermont, was hired to plan the park, which by the following April was known as Mill Race Park, as it is today. Apparently, the people in the new Tipton Park subdivision on the north side of the city weren't too keen on their name being used for the new park. The area had been known by several names: Riverfront Park, White River Park, Death Valley Park and the New City Park. A millrace is a narrow current of water that turns a water wheel or a channel conducting water to or from a water wheel. One of these had been in the site during the pioneer days of Columbus and had been used as a point in surveying records.

A group of individuals known as the River Rats spent countless hours turning the area into a park. Carl Miske was known as the Head Rat. He was joined by Lynn Barkhimer, Bob Marshall, Bert Engle, Herb Boeschen and Robert Dunn to form the Mill Race Park Development Committee.

The park was redesigned in 1993 by Michael Van Valkenburgh Associates. *Landscape Management* magazine has recognized the park as one of the top one hundred parks in the nation for design, reputation and accessibility. It includes an eighty-four-foot observation tower, a covered bridge, hiking trails, two lakes, picnic shelters, playground equipment, horseshoe pits, basketball courts and an amphitheater that hosts concerts and performances.

It took years, many more than most residents thought was necessary, to clean up Death Valley. But eventually, the task was completed, giving the city some first-class green space and eradicating one of the city's worst neighborhoods.

3

LOVE AND BULLETS

When Ralph Drake was sober, he was by all accounts an engaging young man, well-liked and respected by nearly everyone he came in contact with. But when he was on the bottle, he was a completely different person.

Ida Ward got to know both sides of Ralph Drake. She fell in love with the sober side; she lost her life to the intoxicated side.

Ward met Drake around 1890, when she went to the general store that he ran in St. Louis Crossing, northeast of Columbus. She was married, had a young girl and was ten years Drake's senior. But her visits to his store became more frequent, and she eventually fell madly in love with him, a fact that did not go unnoticed by many folks

RALPH DRAKE.

An artist's sketch of Ralph Drake, who served seven years in prison for killing Ida Ward. *Courtesy of the* Republic.

in that town. In fact, many wondered if an elopement was planned should she secure a divorce from her husband, John, a farmer.

Eventually, Ward and her husband separated. Shortly thereafter, Drake's store burned down, and the two lost their meeting place. Drake moved to Columbus to live with his mother and brothers on East Tenth Street, and Ward began making regular trips to Columbus.

Ward's parents and close friends urged her to stop seeing Drake, saying it would ruin her and disgrace those around her. But she was blind to his faults and continued the romance. She had been heard on several occasions to say that Drake should marry her and that if he attempted to marry anyone else, she would kill him.

MRS. IDA WARD.

An artist's sketch of Ida Ward, who was killed by Ralph Drake in 1893. *Courtesy of the* Republic.

She filed suit to secure a divorce, but the proceedings had not yet taken place by the time of her death, as her husband didn't want to give her up.

Drake's early years gave no indication that he would one day commit murder. He was the youngest son of John W. and Emaline Drake, both highly esteemed local residents. Ralph's father was a farmer north of Columbus before passing away in 1886, when Ralph was about nineteen years old.

During his time running the store in St. Louis Crossing, Drake was a citizen in good standing and seemed to have a bright future. He never did enjoy good health, however, and turned to whiskey for comfort. He may have lost some of his will to stay sober when his store burned down; he ran with some men who urged him to drink, and "he soon became a slave to liquor," according to the *Republican*.

That Drake had issues with alcohol was well known. Once, he was found lying in the alley behind George I. Winan's store, at 533 Washington Street, so drunk that he couldn't walk. Police picked him up and took him to jail. He was fined thirteen dollars.

Some of Drake's more compassionate friends sent him to a hospital in Plainfield, west of Indianapolis, to be cured of his alcoholism, and for a time, he lost his desire for whiskey. But he started drinking again and was urged to try a treatment offered by Dr. James B. Hudson in Columbus. This also seemed to work.

But on Saturday morning, May 27, 1893, Drake left Hudson's care and resumed drinking. He went home, where his mother had a difficult time keeping him from hurting himself and other members of the family. He was finally subdued and put to bed until the following morning, when he left the house.

About 11:00 p.m. on the night of Monday, May 29, Ralph Drake and Ida Ward entered the Plymate rooming house on Seventh Street, having just left the De Boos restaurant at 633 Jackson Street. The thirty-six-year-old Ward told Mrs. Plymate that she was married to the twenty-six-year-old Drake and that they lived in St. Louis Crossing. Plymate didn't know either of them and rented them a room for a week, which Ward paid for.

The Plymates rented rooms but did not take in boarders, so renters had to get their meals elsewhere and need not be in much contact with them. None of the Plymate family paid much attention to Drake or Ward while they stayed there, although Plymate said she did talk to Ward a bit a few days after they checked in and said the woman seemed cheerful. Plymate asked her what her husband did for a living, and Ward was evasive. But Ward did say that she owned a farm and soon wished to purchase a lot and house.

Plymate said she only saw Drake once during his time there, on Tuesday afternoon, when he and Ward went to dinner together. Two days later, when Plymate next saw the couple together, Ward was minutes from death, and Drake was severely injured.

On that Thursday, June 1, Drake apparently had several drinks in the morning before going to see Hudson about eleven o'clock or so. Hudson had Marion Mooney, another one of his patients and one of Drake's former drinking buddies, meet with Drake at the doctor's office. Hudson hoped that Mooney would help Drake sober up and get out of a bad mood. The pair left together, and Mooney persuaded Drake to go to Drake's mother's house, taking the Maple Grove trolley to get there.

Ralph's mother, who was thought to be the person best able to restrain him, was not home when the men arrived. Ralph went to his room and started looking through his wardrobe. Mooney asked him if he was going away, but Drake said he was not; he only said he wanted to see if his clothes were all right.

Mooney went out of the house to wait for Drake and suddenly heard the distinctive click of a revolver emanate from the house and expected that Drake was going to shoot himself. Mooney found Ralph's brother, Lester

Drake, out in the yard and told Lester that he thought Ralph was crazy. Lester agreed.

Mooney's efforts to lift Drake's spirits proved fruitless. So Mooney left, thinking the family would take care of him. But Drake just changed his clothes and left the house.

While Drake was away from the boardinghouse, Ward told Plymate that she and Drake would like to stay on longer than originally intended.

While the Plymate family was eating dinner about six o'clock that evening, they were horrified to hear three pistol shots, fired in rapid succession, from the upstairs room occupied by the couple. There was a scream and a heavy fall. Within another thirty seconds, two more shots rang out. The family and others in the house raced to the room where Drake and Ward were staying.

Plymate checked the door, but it was locked. She ran into the street and yelled for Dr. George T. McCoy, the county health officer. McCoy came quickly, ran upstairs and pulled himself up to peer through a transom at the top of the door. He could see Ward lying in agony and Drake sitting nearby. McCoy called to Drake to unlock the door, which he did.

The scene was ghastly. On the floor, with her head resting on two suits of men's clothes, lay the dying Ward. She gasped for breath while blood flowed into her mouth and throat, choking her. Her skull was shattered, and observers noted that they could see her brain. One button had burst off her dress; she had one shoe off, and the other was untied. It was apparent that she had been shot at close range and rolled about a few feet from where she had initially fallen to the floor.

To her left was Ralph Drake in a kneeling position with his elbows on a cane-bottomed chair and face in his hands. Shortly after the door was opened, Drake tried to rise but immediately fell backward next to Ward. Turning to those in the room, he yelled out, "Oh, kill me, please! Please kill me, but let her alone!"

Within thirty minutes, Ward was dead and Drake was on his way to the county jail.

A late-model .32-caliber Smith & Wesson revolver with its chamber emptied was found in the room. Three of the balls had passed through Ward's head; one went through Drake's head just below his ear and passed along the skull and out the top of his head, without injuring the skull. The fifth ball was lodged in a door casing. The morning after the shooting, Drake sat on a stool in a corner of his jail cell with his face buried in his hands. He was "pale and haggard and the perfect picture of despair," with two white cloths wrapping his wounds. He refused to talk, except to say that he did the

LOVE AND BULLETS!

A Mixture of the Two Causes Mrs. Ida Ward To Lose Her Life.

A Horrible Murder Committed in a Columbus Lodging House.

Ralph Drake, the Murderer, in Jail, the Picture of Dispair

An Untrue Wife Goes Disgraced to the Grave, but Her Husband Loved Her Still.

Women, Wine and Pistols Dangerous to Fool With. Grand Jury Called in Special Session.

Ralph Drake was found guilty of murder in the second degree for the killing of Ida Ward. *Courtesy of the* Republic.

shooting and wished he'd killed himself. He refused to talk at the preliminary hearing that afternoon.

While Drake waited in jail, the woman he shot was buried at Flatrock Baptist Cemetery, between Columbus and St. Louis Crossing, with what was described as a large attendance at her funeral. A few days later, Drake was officially charged with murder following coroner Frederick Falk's findings. The prosecuting attorney, William Waltman, immediately filed an affidavit charging Drake with first-degree murder.

Drake's appearance in Justice John W. Morgan's court on the morning of June 6 drew quite a crowd. At ten o'clock, city marshal George Lewellen led Drake from the jail to the courthouse, the accused wearing leg irons, a bandage over his head wounds and his familiar gold-rimmed glasses. Devoid of emotion, he was followed by two brothers, Frank and Lester, and an uncle, John L. Graves.

Drake's defense team consisted of attorneys Marshall Hacker and Charles Remy. David Emig was retained to prosecute Drake. The judge didn't set bail at that time due to Drake's weakened physical condition. And since the state had not read the evidence yet, the trial was continued to the next day.

When Drake came before the judge again, the scene was similar to that of the previous day, with a large throng of onlookers present and Drake in an emotionless state. He spoke only in whispers to his attorneys, while his brothers drew near to hear what he was saying. The case was submitted only on the coroner's evidence, and since that showed no malice intended, the judge had no option but to allow bail, which he set at $10,000. Had it been proven that Drake had threatened Ward or they had quarreled on the day of the shooting, the judge might have had the option to refuse bail. The prosecuting attorney argued that the simple fact that there was a murder showed malice, but the judge disagreed.

Even though Drake's friends could have raised the money necessary to get him out of jail until his trial, nobody did so, fearing he might commit suicide if released. That fear caused some members of his family and friends to try to get him declared insane. Proceedings toward that goal took place on July 3 before Justice William Warren Stader. Drake's mother, brother Frank, Dr. Hudson and George W. Caldwell testified on his behalf. They all said that Drake had become more morose in jail and claimed he would be better off in an asylum.

Stader agreed and had Drake committed to the Central Insane Asylum in Indianapolis. The decision didn't sit well with the general public in Columbus, but the insanity proceedings would not prevent Drake from being tried for murder in the future.

It seemed to be the general opinion of county residents that people who had committed the type of murder that Drake did had gone without enough punishment in the past. It was hoped by many that he would return for trial in the fall and be found guilty.

Drake, indeed, was returned to Columbus in late September, although he still refused to talk to anyone and did not seem to care much about his future. He even appeared uncomfortable around those whom he should have counted as friends.

His next appearance in court was on October 6, but the trial didn't start until the following May. Drake's attorneys asked for some continuances and a change of venue, saying that their client could not possibly get a fair trial in Bartholomew County. The case was moved to Greensburg, in Decatur County.

A year in confinement had done wonders for Drake's health. He had gotten his appetite back and put on some weight. He had also been off the liquor. He seemed cheerful, although he still only spoke when spoken to. When Drake took his seat in the courtroom, he was no more than ten feet from John Ward, the husband of the woman he had killed. Remy pointed out in his opening remarks that the defense would show that Drake was not guilty by reason of insanity.

The trial lasted about ten days, and seventy-five witnesses testified.

During the trial, McCoy testified that on the night of the shooting, Drake confessed, saying, "There is nothing to tell you, doctor, nothing. You see it all. I want to die; let me die….I told her I would kill her and then kill myself, and I have failed to do so."

Ida Ward's mother, Mrs. George Cook, created a stir with her testimony that day. Instead of answering the questions she was asked, she made whatever statements she pleased and didn't seem to care when admonished by the court. She did say that a few days before the shooting, Drake came to her house and left with her daughter, saying, "I am a gentleman and have money to take care for your daughter, and I am going to take her now. It is now or never."

One of the witnesses described how Drake wasn't always able to keep his attention on his work. Caldwell, a partner with Drake's brother Lester in the real estate business, said that Drake worked for their company for a while. He was to dump dirt from a scraper the company was using to grade a new addition to the city. He often paid little attention to how he was to do the job, left the job for others to do and sometimes just sat down and stared off into space, Caldwell said. He added that he saw Drake on the day of the shooting at his mother's house and thought he looked wild and pale. He said he considered Drake to be of unsound mind that day.

One of Drake's star witnesses was Dr. J.Y. Kennedy of Flat Rock. Kennedy was a close friend of Drake's—just about his only companion for a three-year period—and had also practiced medicine at St. Louis Crossing, treating Drake for delirium tremens, a rapid onset of confusion usually caused by withdrawal from alcohol. Kennedy had sometimes seen Drake pour down eight alcoholic drinks in a matter of moments and considered him of unsound mind for several years.

When Drake drank to excess, he would claim friends and acquaintances were out to get him and conversed with them when they were not present, according to Kennedy. At the request of Drake's family, Kennedy took Drake on an extended trip to Colorado and other places out West about seventeen months before the shooting.

Once, in Colorado, while the pair was passing a house, Drake remarked that his father had taken him there many years ago and he had gone down the mountain into the mist. Drake had never been to that state before, Kennedy said.

On the way back home from that trip, Kennedy took Drake to Dwight, Illinois, and left him at Keeley Institute to undergo the famed Keeley Treatment, or Gold Treatment, as it was called. Shortly after he returned to this area, Drake moved in with his mother. Kennedy concluded that Drake's mind had gotten worse over the past three years, with strong drink being the major factor.

Z.T. Sweeney, a well-respected minister at Tabernacle Church of Christ (now First Christian

The Reverend Z.T. Sweeney, a well-respected man in Columbus who had at various times tried to counsel Ralph Drake. *Bartholomew County Historical Society.*

Church), said he had known Drake for at least ten years and had sometimes discussed with him his spiritual and mental state. He also considered Drake unsound.

Hudson testified that when Drake showed up at his office the day of the shooting, "He was morose, nervous and I feared that if he got out upon the street he would injure someone. He wanted to go but I prevented it."

When Mooney came to the doctor's office, Hudson told him to take Drake home. "From what I saw of Drake, and know of his physical condition, he is a person of unsound mind," Hudson concluded.

Dr. J.F. Wright, who was Ralph Drake's father's physician for twenty-five years and well acquainted with several of Ralph's uncles, said that all these men suffered from an unsound mind to one degree or another as they aged. Wright, whose forty-year medical career included fourteen months in France studying insanity, said Ralph was of unsound mind.

By the time the defense had finished making its case, it had called forty witnesses, all of whom said Drake was of unsound mind. Drake did not take the stand. The prosecution, meanwhile, focused mainly on men who had business dealings with Drake. They all said he seemed of sound mind when they interacted with him.

Many thought that Drake would get off on the insanity plea, but the jury saw things otherwise and found him guilty of murder in the second degree. He was ordered to be sentenced to the fullest extent of the law, which meant life in prison. The second-degree charge meant that malice was presumed and premeditation was not taken into account. Drake had been indicted for first-degree murder, but no malice was proven during the trial.

Drake was unmoved by the verdict, maintaining the same degree of indifference he had since the day after the shooting.

There had never been a case emanating from Bartholomew County that had attracted the amount of attention that this one did. The costs of the case were tremendous for the time. The stenographer's notes came to 1,600 typewritten pages. At forty cents each, the stenographer would get $640 in case the transcript was needed. The amount of money paid to the witnesses totaled $3,500.

Drake's attorneys sought a new trial at the state supreme court. That motion was put on hold when someone stole part of the record of the proceedings. The appeal papers were eventually filed in early December. The supreme court heard the case in October the following year, affirming the lower court's decision.

In the meantime, Drake was sent to the state prison in Jeffersonville before being transferred to the facility in Michigan City on April 12, 1897, when the two prisons traded several hundred inmates. A total of 378 convicts were shifted from the southern prison to the northern one. Among those prisoners moving were two other Columbus men, John Petilliot and Cy Brown, both of whom had been convicted of murdering their wives. When the prisoner train passed through towns, large throngs of people gathered to view it.

As the train rumbled past the Columbus depot (it didn't stop anywhere along its route) at 10:10 a.m., John Petilliot reportedly smiled when he saw his old bird dog, Dude, who had been brought to the station. A similar train traveling southbound with prisoners from Michigan City to Jeffersonville went through Columbus later that day.

Drake assumed he would be in the Michigan City prison for the rest of his days. But behind the scenes, friends and relatives, especially those of Drake's mother, started pushing for his parole. Early in the 1900s, the state board of pardons recommended his release. But two different governors, Winton T. Durbin and J. Frank Hanly, denied Drake his freedom.

The matter came up before the board of pardons again in April 1909. By that time, Drake had reportedly been a model prisoner for several years and was the head of the prison's tailoring department, which made all of the prisoners' clothes. Indiana also had a new governor, which gave Drake a much better shot at getting released.

Governor Thomas R. Marshall had said at the beginning of his term that he would accept all recommendations by the board of pardons. And he kept his promise. About a week after receiving the board's recommendation that Drake be paroled, Marshall signed it.

Ralph Drake, who had spent nearly sixteen years incarcerated in either an asylum, county jail or state prison, left Michigan City the morning of May 11, 1909. He hopped aboard a train and headed home to see his mother and the rest of his friends and family. The warden sent word via telegram to Drake's mother that her son would be arriving in Columbus that day. Emaline Drake supposed that meant her son would arrive on the Pennsylvania Railroad train shortly after five o'clock that evening, providing her "a ray of sunshine in her darkened life." It was said that "for years she had been waiting for just such word, and the news was as welcome as any she had ever before received," a story in the *Republican* said.

But it would not be a happy homecoming for Drake and his mother.

Emaline Drake, a seventy-six-year-old woman who had not seen her son in twelve years, went to the depot with her grandson, John Drake, and a friend,

MRS. DRAKE DIES WHILE HASTENING TO MEET SON

HORRIBLE DEATH OF LOCAL WOMAN

Mrs. Drake on Her Way to Meet Son Ralph Who was Due from Prison.

WAS PAROLED TUESDAY

MOTHER HAD NOT SEEN SON FOR TWELVE YEARS AND WAS OBLIVIOUS OF ENGINE AS SHE HURRIED TO CROSS THE TRACK.

Mrs. Emaline Drake, who lived on east Tenth street, was almost instantly killed by a Pennsylvania lines passenger engine at the Pennsylvania passenger station Tuesday afternoon about 5 o'clock. Her death came as she was on her way to meet her son, Ralph Drake, who had been paroled Tuesday from the Michigan City prison, where he had been serving a life sentence. Intent on meeting the

south of the station, where it is left nights, was being taken to the round house near the bridge and was running north at a slow rate of speed. It was the intention of the engineer to make the switch near the water pipe, north of the station, and then head down the main line and thus be out of the way. Engineer Tyrrell did not see the women and the boy start to cross the track and he did not stop until he heard the screams of people who were standing near. When the engine was brought to a stop the tender had passed completely over Mrs. Drake's body, as had also one track of the engine. Efforts were made to pull the woman from under the engine, but it was seen at a glance that she was dead and the body could not be moved. The engine remained stationary and jacks had to be used to raise it high enough to remove the body. Deputy Coroner Frank L. Flanigan was called and took charge of the mangled corpse. The engine remained where it had been stopped until the place was viewed and then it was allowed to proceed.

Mrs. Drake was horribly mangled by the tender and engine, the left leg was ground to a pulp and the left foot cut entirely off. The right leg was cut almost in two and mangled and one set of wheels passed over the waist, crushing the body terribly. The left arm was practically cut off and the face was cut and bruised where the woman had been pressed against the crossties and gravel. One shoe was found containing a portion of the left foot and Mrs. Drake's false teeth were also found lying beside the rails

Ralph Drake's mother was hit by a train and killed just ten minutes before he arrived in Columbus to see her following his release from prison. *Courtesy of the* Republic.

Julia Nading. Emaline Drake drove her buggy from her home and hitched her horse at the Martin Saloon on the east side of Jackson Street. She soon heard the train whistle and was intent on being on the platform to greet her son when he got off the train. She and her companions crossed Jackson Street and had only the width of the Madison branch tracks to cross before getting to safety.

But in their haste, they didn't hear another train moving along the Madison spur from the south. The train, which had sat south of the station the previous night, was traveling northbound slowly to a roundhouse near the bridge over the White River. The engineer didn't see anyone crossing the track, and the engine slammed into Emaline Drake and clipped Nading. The boy jumped to safety.

When he heard the screams of those who witnessed the event, the driver halted the train, which had rolled over Mrs. Drake and stopped on top of her. She was killed instantly. Jacks had to be used to lift the train so that the body could be removed. Witnesses saw a horrid sight. Her left foot had been cut off, and her right leg was cut almost in two. Her false teeth were found lying beside the rails.

Meanwhile, Ralph Drake was unaware of what had happened to his mother. He wasn't on the Pennsylvania Railroad train. He arrived on the interurban instead, getting off on Washington Street within ten minutes after the train accident several blocks away. He hadn't told anyone how and when he would be arriving, so he wasn't expecting anyone to meet him.

Drake got on the trolley to take him to his mother's house, where he assumed he would find his nearest and dearest friend. But when he arrived, family friend B.M. Hutchins caught Drake before he got to the door and broke the news to him that the most influential and important person in his life had been killed while she was just minutes from seeing him. Weeping uncontrollably, Drake staggered into the house and sank down like a broken man.

Emaline Drake had been a lifelong resident of Bartholomew County and was well-respected, charitable and kind. Her death at any time would have brought much grief from many citizens. But the circumstances in which her passing occurred became one of the most heart-rending stories that the county had ever endured.

Such a blow would have likely caused Ralph Drake to go back to the bottle or do himself in when he was younger. But he emerged from prison a much stronger man. At the age of forty-two, he had finally gotten his life on track.

The following year, he married Mary Lortz of Nortonburg, northeast of Columbus. He took a job with his brothers' company, Caldwell & Drake Iron Works, becoming treasurer and eventually co-owner. He was a member of the local Christian church, attended services regularly and took an active interest in politics, once running as a Democrat for ward committeeman.

In 1912, he was pardoned by Marshall. He continued to live in his mother's house, 1628 East Tenth Street, eventually buying the place, until his death from heart trouble and other diseases on December 11, 1924, at the age of fifty-seven.

He never did say publicly whether Ward had agreed to a murder-suicide pact or if the idea was all his. But Ralph Drake did serve as an example of how a man can be a completely different person when not under the control of alcohol.

4

WHITECAPPERS AND THE KKK

*O*ver its various incarnations, the Ku Klux Klan has provided America with one of its most recognizable symbols of intolerance, hatred and fear.

In Indiana, the Klan wielded a great deal of political power in the 1920s. An unmasked "kinder and gentler" Klan, as some members touted it in the 1960s and '70s, caused quite a stir locally by starting a Columbus chapter and marching around the courthouse in 1977.

But before this area experienced the white hoods of the KKK, there was another group of hooded individuals that dispensed its own brand of justice during the second half of the nineteenth century and the beginning of the twentieth: Whitecappers, or Whitecaps.

The Indiana whitecapping movement was thought to have started in 1837. The first Whitecap encounters were generally aimed at those who went against a community's values. Men who neglected or abused their families, people who showed excessive laziness and women who had children out of wedlock were all possible targets.

As the groups became more numerous and popular, they started lynching criminals or suspected criminals. Race and creed didn't seem to be a factor in the Whitecap lynchings. Between 1860 and 1910, at least sixty-eight people were lynched by Whitecappers; twenty were black, and forty-eight were white. In all cases, the victims had been suspected criminals, almost all of whom were in state custody when they were killed.

An illustration depicting a whitecapping incident in Indiana. *From* Frank Leslie's Illustrated Newspaper.

Whitecappers didn't operate as heavily in Bartholomew County as they did in some nearby counties, especially to the south and west. But a few newsworthy whitecapping cases did come out of the area.

One of the first involved a dozen people from Jackson Township going to trial in county court before Judge Thomas F. Hord in October 1893. They were accused of whipping Mary K. Schrader, a wife and mother of five who lived on a farm near Waymansville, southwest of Columbus.

She said she heard a grunting noise outside the house about midnight or so. She asked her husband, Andrew, to check it out. When he opened the door, he yelled, "Murder! Murder!" A moment later, a few men—faces and hands blackened—held revolvers to his face. They chased Mary and put part of her dress in her mouth to muffle the cries as they took turns whipping her.

She yelled as best she could, "My God, my God, have mercy on me! Have mercy on us all!"

The motive for the attack, she said, was misguided revenge. For a time, her father-in-law, John J. Schrader, lived with the family. The elder Schrader told relatives that his daughter-in-law had treated him poorly. The relatives and others were the alleged attackers, and Mary alleged that marital issues between her and her husband was the real reason that caused her father-in-law to seek revenge. That trial ended in a hung jury, but a subsequent trial convicted one man, sending him to prison for a year.

A branch of Whitecappers that operated west of Columbus near the Bartholomew-Brown County line made news in July 1894 by taking Perry Bloomfield and his family from their home and whipping them "unmercifully." The Whitecappers shot one man in the heel when he attempted to flee and whipped him. No reason for the attack was given, but the group told the family to leave the area.

There were quite a few reports of Whitecappers whipping and beating people in Brown County in the early 1900s. Rarely, if ever, were the perpetrators indicted. They always seemed to have witnesses who said they were not at the scenes of the crime, and the victims were often reluctant to testify and moved away soon after an attack.

The Whitecappers did not endear themselves to the general populace, and on October 9, 1902, the *Republican* came down hard on their practices. "The press must stand out boldly for law and order and suppression of the mob spirit," it said, noting that law enforcement had been doing a good job and that the people favored law enforcement over vigilante practices.

In June 1907, Thomas VanEst, a forty-two-year-old carpenter and blacksmith at South Bethany, a town twelve miles west–southwest of

Thomas VanEst was the victim of a Bartholomew County whitecapping attack in 1907. *Courtesy of the* Republic.

Columbus that no longer exists, was dragged from his bed just after midnight, taken by surrey to a remote place in the woods and whipped by seven or eight men. He said he'd been told this was done because he had been mean to his wife and pushed her down. He denied this charge to his attackers, which brought him more lashes from a hickory switch and a heavy buggy whip. He was then told to leave his wife and move far away and never come back or "the job would be finished."

VanEst, whose wife and three children were also home at the time, said that he was able to identify nearly all the men who whitecapped him, as the moon was shining brightly, there was a hole in the binder twine sack put over his head and the men were unmasked. He said they were all related to him or his wife. It later came out that family members had been squabbling over an inheritance, which VanEst suggested was the real reason for the attack.

Charges of engaging in riotous conspiracy were filed in Columbus against the alleged perpetrators. Known as the Whitecap Law, it was passed in 1899 and amended in 1905. It said that if three or more people conspired for the purpose of performing an illegal act at night or to do illegal activities "while wearing white caps, masks or otherwise being disguised," they should be judged guilty of riotous conspiracy. The penalty for conviction was two to ten years in state prison as well as a fine of up to $2,000. The law was rarely enforced, though.

VanEst's attackers were not easy to bring to trial, and a reward of fifty dollars apiece was offered for their arrest. The county commissioners offered the reward because they didn't want Bartholomew County to be known as a county "disgraced by whitecapping outrages."

Two of the eight accused, David Fox and Jacob Kirk, were convicted. The men petitioned for a new trial, which dragged through 1908 and most of 1909. At one point, it was suggested that the state drop the charges, but it had too much evidence. The state finally agreed to drop any punishment if the men would plead guilty. In late November 1909, more than two years after the incident, the men changed their pleas to guilty and took a suspended sentence.

The Indiana whitecapping movement died out in the early 1910s. It wasn't long before the Columbus area was afflicted by another pack of the hooded kind, the Ku Klux Klan.

The KKK originated in Tennessee following the Civil War and was suppressed around 1871 through federal law enforcement.

The Klan was revived in Georgia in 1915 and flourished nationwide in the early and mid-1920s, particularly in urban areas of the Midwest and West. This version adopted a modern business system of using full-time paid recruiters and appealed to new members as a fraternal, patriotic organization. However, after members joined, many of them found out the KKK had more than just fraternizing on its mind. It opposed blacks, Catholics, Jews and newer immigrants, especially those from southern Europe. The Klan adopted a standard white costume with hoods and masks.

Bartholomew County wasn't as attracted to the second version of the Klan as some other areas of Indiana. And the organization's first attempt to recruit here was met with a cold shoulder, partly because Bartholomew County tended to leave matters of law enforcement to the proper officials.

Still, the KKK eventually caught on here.

Columbus saw one of its first public KKK activities on the afternoon of Sunday, April 2, 1922, when Dr. Charles Lewis Fowler of Atlanta made an open-air address on Fourth Street between Washington and Jackson Streets after being denied access to city hall to talk the previous day. The board of public works had originally allowed Fowler to rent a room in city hall to explain the purposes and operations of the Ku Klux Klan. A protest by residents had caused a reversal by the board the day of the scheduled talk.

Fowler's public address attracted a small but attentive crowd. He appealed to residents' sense of "Americanism," declaring that the KKK's slogan was "America for Americans and Americans for America." He said the only people eligible for membership were white Protestant Anglo-Saxons born in this country, saying Negroes were not eligible because the white race should have supremacy and Catholics and Jews were prohibited because those religions had their own organizations.

Following the speech, a number of residents signed a petition presented to the board of public works that Fowler be allowed to speak at city hall on Monday night. That morning, the petition was granted. Not everyone who was in favor of allowing Fowler to speak at city hall was in favor of the Ku Klux Klan, but some were simply in favor of allowing all organizations the opportunity to present their views.

Fowler, the founder of Lanier University in Atlanta, and for years, its president, attracted more than six hundred people to his lecture. The *Evening Republican* attributed the big crowd to the fact that Fowler had previously been denied permission to lecture. The crowd replied with enthusiasm when Fowler made remarks with which it agreed. It also showed disapproval when Fowler spoke of the exclusion of three sets of Americans from his organization. Fowler closed by saying that local Klansmen, unknown to the general population, would be contacting people favorable to the KKK to invite them to join.

When the meeting broke up about 9:20 p.m., several groups formed near city hall to discuss what had been said. Few people voiced opposition to most of what Fowler had said, but the method they had heard the Klan use in other areas to achieve its goals concerned many.

By the end of the month, Bartholomew County saw its first official Klan meeting, with more than one hundred members of the new local branch, along with another thirty-five candidates, gathering in a grove north of Columbus on April 28. Each member wore a white mask. The meeting was described as spectacular and mysterious.

Free Lecture--Tonight--City Hall--7:30

DR. C. LEWIS FOWLER

Founder and for years president of the Lanier University, Atlanta, Ga., is to give a FREE LECTURE on "America for Americans" under the auspices of the

KU KLUX KLAN

No admission charges or free will offering of any nature, and OPEN TO THE PUBLIC, regardless of SEX or CREED. You have heard the Klan attacked and heard various charges made against it and in all fairness and justice you should hear the facts about this wonderful American organization.

A day after making a speech on Fourth Street because he had been denied a chance to make one in city hall, Louis K. Fowler was allowed to speak on the Ku Klux Klan at city hall in April 1922. *Courtesy of the* Republic.

Local sentiment became divided on the invisible empire, which often publicly stated it had no quarrel with people of other religions or races, but only sought to, as one letter writer to the *Evening Republican* said in May 1922, "suppress graft in government, prevent the causes of mob violence and lynchings, establish sensible immigration laws, keep church and state separate, and ensure a freedom of press and speech that does not imperil the government or cherished public institutions." The letter was signed "A Klansman."

A rebuttal appeared in the next day's paper from "A Christian," wanting to know why, if the KKK was interested in such values as chivalry, character, protection of home and patriotism, it had to do so behind masks, when all major religions taught such things in the open. The writer also asked why anyone would try to stir up intolerance against three groups of people that had bravely served their country during World War I.

In May, local Catholic priest Father C.P. Barron and a prominent member of his church awoke one morning to see large red placards attached to trees in front of their homes that read, "Here yesterday, here today, here tomorrow, Ku Klux Klan." Identical placards were placed at two other locations in Columbus, and some had been seen in other areas of Bartholomew County.

Two members of the local KKK chapter created a stir on a Sunday morning in July when they entered the United Brethren Church during the opening hymn and handed the pastor an envelope with five twenty-dollar bills and a note inside. They did this in full Klan garb, including masks and hoods, did not speak and left immediately afterward. The note said that the money

The Ku Klux Klan held a small rally in downtown Columbus in 1922. *Bartholomew County Historical Society.*

was to go toward a memorial fund for a recently deceased member of the congregation and included a note of thanks for the good work the church was doing. About a year later, a women's organization of the Klan made its first public appearance in Columbus, donating fifty dollars to the same memorial.

The local Klan held what is believed to be its first march in Columbus on Saturday, October 14, 1922: seven white-gowned and masked members of the group walked up and down the city streets encouraging people to attend a talk at city hall that night by Klan lecturer L.A. Brown of Atlanta.

The Klan received support by doing good deeds around the community.

In September 1922, Klansmen gave a needy seventy-seven-year-old East Columbus woman and widow of a Methodist minister "an elaborate donation" of fuel, food and $1,500 in cash that would sustain her for the entire winter. Klan members, both regular and junior members, met at midnight on Christmas Eve in Donner Park for several years to conduct Christmas rituals. The women's auxiliary, dressed in their robes, spent the evening passing out food baskets to the needy. Both white and black families were included, the *Evening Republican* noted.

The local KKK, which eventually had its headquarters in the Pfeiffer Building at 315 Washington Street, helped local authorities raid illegal booze sellers and donated twenty-five copies of the 1924 *Log*, Columbus High School's yearbook, to needy students.

The Columbus church community expressed varying opinions of the Klan in its early days here.

Evangelist A.P. Renn delivered a glowing picture of the Klansman as a true American during a revival meeting at First Baptist Church in November 1922. The meeting was highlighted by the unfurling of a large American flag at the beginning of his sermonette and the display of a "fiery" cross at the end. The lights in the sanctuary were turned off, and red electric lights were shown on the cross. Renn's words riled up a lot of folks, whether they were pro-Klan, anti-Klan or on the fence.

Plenty of other local religious leaders preached opposing messages. Despite the fact that most of the country's major Christian religions either officially or unofficially denounced the Klan and its actions as going against the teachings of Christ, the KKK continued to use Christianity as an excuse for its actions as well as a drawing card for attracting members.

The KKK also threw its support toward political candidates, despite the fact that some of the candidates didn't necessarily want it. One example came in the November 1922 election when the local Klan sent sample ballots to homes with certain candidates marked as approved by its organization. One of the candidates, Charles F. Remy of Indianapolis, who was running for the Republican nod for judge of the appellate court of Indiana, cringed at the news the KKK had supported him.

"They are not endorsing me because I endorsed them, for I do not approve of such organizations," Remy said. "They are fighting my opponent because he is a Knight of Columbus and yet I know him to be a fine man."

The national Klan received press for both good and bad deeds during these years. In addition to the donations the group made to needy residents, local papers also reported on such KKK doings as lynchings and Indiana imperial wizard Edward Young Clarke getting indicted for misuse of the U.S. mail system and resigning his post.

In late 1922, the American Theatre on Fifth Street offered *The Mysterious Eyes of the Ku Klux Klan*, a film that purported to be the only one ever made to positively tell the inner workings of the Klan. The theater scheduled six shows on Saturday, November 11, to accommodate the crowds.

In December, four men thought to be Klansmen erected a fifteen-foot-tall cross near the fountain in the center of Commercial Park at the southeast corner of Fifth and Franklin Streets. They ignited it, and it burned for ten minutes. A similar scene took place about a week later on a vacant lot on Washington Street between Fifth and Sixth, leading the American Equality League to take out an ad in the *Evening Republican* to calm fears locals might have.

"Do not be afraid or terrorized," the ad stated. "There are enough sensible citizens left to protect you and see that the law and order of our country is honored....[O]ur government of the people, by the people and for the people" would not be replaced by "a government of the Klan, by the Klan and for the Klan."

Within a few weeks, a chapter of the American Equality League organized in Columbus.

The Klan, however, continued to become more accepted in Indiana. From July 1922 to July 1923, under the leadership of new grand dragon D.C. Stephenson, an average of 2,000 new members joined the Indiana Klan each week, giving the state the most Klansmen in the nation. At one point, the Indiana Klan boasted 250,000 members, an estimated 30 percent of the native-born white men here. And by 1925, more than half the elected members of the state's general assembly, and the governor, were Klan members.

Bartholomew County's views of the Klan were not much different than the rest of Indiana during this time. Some pointed to the good the organization did and the values it said it supported; others pointed to the fear tactics and mystery employed by the group. And while reports reached this area of alleged tortures and murders at the hands of the organization in other parts of the nation, the KKK became more visible and added members in the county.

About 250 Kluxers, as they were sometimes called, marched in Columbus on May 26, 1923. That was well short of the 1,000 promised in advertisements leading up to the event. The festivities were curtailed when many of the robes that were to be shipped here for Klansmen to wear were mistakenly sent to Columbus, Ohio. That made for a smaller parade but a much larger audience, as members of the order who did not have robes blended in with the crowd. The parade marched to Commercial Park, where the Muncie Klan band performed.

Even while the Klan enjoyed great success in the Indiana political arena during this time, the organization was not without its detractors.

C.B. Cooper, a local attorney, took an opportunity to speak against the Klan during the proceedings of the Bartholomew County teachers institute on August 29, 1923. In that same month, Edinburgh's Billie Hill, a candidate for the House of Representatives from the Fourth District, which included Bartholomew County, purchased ads in local newspapers explaining that despite his stance against many Klan ideologies, he felt he would still make a good selection. He then gave several anti-Klan speeches.

The first reported incidents of physical confrontation in the county resulting from Klan activities occurred during a September 29, 1923 KKK parade in Columbus. It was held in conjunction with an all-day and evening homecoming at the county fairgrounds on Twenty-Fifth Street. Between fifteen and twenty thousand people converged on downtown for the event, in which several hundred Klansmen participated, making it the largest such parade in county history to that point. Washington Street between Second and Eighth Streets was overstuffed with humanity. Included were two large floats; two bands; a drum corps; cars decorated in red, white and blue; and men and women of the Klan.

Fights started when an onlooker was jumped on when he did not remove his hat when the American flag passed by him near Fourth and Washington Streets. Others joined in, and a free-for-all erupted. The parade had to be halted until order was restored. Several other similar incidents occurred, but police were not summoned and no arrests were made.

In March 1924, Bartholomew County found itself with the fewest candidates for office since the primary system started. Anyone declaring candidacy would be forced by public demand to state whether they were pro- or anti-Klan, so some candidates filed at the eleventh hour. It was said party lines would have little to do with the election outcomes; they would be decided by Klan lines instead.

An editorial in the May 3 *Evening Republican* ahead of the primary tried to remind people the Klan issue was not the only issue on which they should be casting their ballots. "Too much stress has been put on the Klan-anti-Klan issue as far as politics in Bartholomew County is concerned in this campaign. In all reality it is not an issue at all. The issue, now and always, is the man himself!" The editorial said people should get to know the integrity, honesty and competency of the candidates and vote accordingly.

When the votes were tallied, all the Republican candidates who had advertised themselves as anti-Klan candidates were victorious. Meanwhile, all the Democratic winners were said to be either Klansmen or Klan sympathizers. That meant a Klan versus anti-Klan November general election for every office.

Residents who ventured downtown on the morning of October 29 witnessed two black men arguing the pros and cons of the Ku Klux Klan at Fifth and Washington Streets. Elmer Goens of the Jones & Kleinhens barbershop took the anti-Klan view, while H.F. Smith, a schoolteacher from Princeton, Indiana, spoke in favor of the Klan. Smith was in town to speak at a meeting at city hall designed to encourage black residents to vote for pro-Klan candidates in the state election. He was joined by Eugene Armstrong, a real estate agent from Indianapolis. But no blacks attended, only two to three hundred whites.

The local results of the November 4 election favored Klan candidates in six out of eight races, five of the winners being Democrats and one being a Klan-sympathetic Republican. County voters supported anti-Klan gubernatorial candidate Hugh McCullouch easily over Ed Jackson, a Klansman who won the statewide vote.

Shortly after the election, though, the Klan started losing its influence in Indiana. Corrupt and ineffective leadership was blamed. But the biggest blow was Indiana Grand Wizard D.C. Stephenson's conviction for the savage rape and murder of Madge Oberholtzer, the head of the state's commission to combat illiteracy. News of the attack was reported at the end of March 1925, and Stevenson was in prison at Michigan City by the end of November.

After Stephenson was denied a pardon by Jackson, the man he had supported for governor, Stephenson turned on his former Klansmen and the politicians they had bribed. Some of the politicians went to trial, and many were forced to resign on bribery charges. Stephenson spent thirty-one years in prison on second-degree murder charges before being paroled. Jackson was also deemed guilty of bribery, but the statute of limitations had run out on his activity. He did not seek reelection when his term expired.

By the middle of April 1925, Klan/anti-Klan tensions in Bartholomew County had cooled off, too. The city campaigns for the spring election were said to have much milder feelings than the previous year's county election. Two anti-Klan men, Stanley J. Cooper and Cassius B. Cooper, won their parties' nomination for Columbus mayor, ensuring the Klan would not be an issue in the general election come November.

And the local Klan had separated into two factions, one using the former name, the other going by the Columbus Boosters Club, meaning Klan members were now arguing with each other instead of against anti-Klan foes. No longer was the Klan a major force in the local or state political arena.

Factions of the Klan, or similar organizations, existed across the country through the Great Depression, during World War II, into the Cold War and beyond. But it wasn't until the 1960s that the Klan revived to national prominence again.

Changing social values, the Vietnam War, urban riots and industrial restructuring caused widespread economic and social disruption during the 1960s and '70s. And the Klan was there to spread its message of intolerance once again. By mid-1965, Indiana residents were being recruited by the KKK.

Organized Klan activity in Bartholomew County was virtually absent until 1972, when Klan members passed out literature in Columbus. One piece "derogatory to a race" was not passed out at the request of Mayor Max Andress. The first official Klan charter issued for Bartholomew County since the 1920s came in February 1975. It wasn't long before the organization started making its presence known in a threatening way.

Winston Napier of Indianapolis hands literature on the KKK to a passing motorist at Second and Washington Streets in September 1972. *Courtesy of the* Republic.

On the night of April 9, 1975, the Klan left a calling card in the form of a four-and-a-half-foot-tall wooden cross tacked with KKK cards and slogans on an interracial Columbus couple's lawn. Mike Shipley, a twenty-six-year-old black man, found the cross planted in his yard near Cherry Street and Illinois Avenue about 8:30 p.m. His twenty-year-old wife, Sherri, was white. He and his wife had graduated from Columbus High School, and they had a four-month-old child. The cross bore notes that said the "KKK is watching you" and "Race Mixing is a Disease—Let's Cure the Sick Ones."

Shipley said this was the second time his home had been targeted, but he thought a note attached to his front door with KKK slogans had been a joke. He said Columbus might be seen as a model city, but blacks did have to deal with discrimination here. He said he wasn't looking for trouble but would not be intimidated into moving or changing his lifestyle.

An editorial in the *Republic* two days later denounced the Klan's action: "We cannot believe this community is ready to tolerate Ku Klux Klan crosses placed on front lawns whether in the dead of night or in the last moments of spring twilight as this one was....It is not funny and it must not be tolerated."

A local radio talk show that featured four local Klansmen caused a stir in May. Two unidentified Klansmen were guests on WCSI's *Open Line* program in the early afternoon of May 6. Shortly after the show ended, a group of about ten black residents assembled near the entrance to the radio station, at Fifth and Washington Streets, where they argued with seven Klansmen. Police were called, but there were no incidents.

The group of blacks—which included Mike Shipley, who carried the cross that had been placed in his yard less than a month prior—went to city hall to see the mayor and then to the Law Enforcement Building to see police chief David Hilycord. Neither official was in.

They criticized WCSI for not inviting some of them to appear on the show with the KKK to give their viewpoints. "They teach kids to hate," Lawrence Davis said. "If we didn't say anything, they'd be back in three more weeks. We're interested in not seeing them here at all."

James Kauper, station manager, said the Klan had asked to be on the show, and he had hoped that by putting them on, "the Klan would reveal itself for what it is." Chuck Underwood, host of the *Open Line* program, said he would try to arrange a time for blacks to offer their views during a future show.

In early December, the *Republic* interviewed two local Klansmen, who wished to remain anonymous. They spoke of the new Klan, a kinder and gentler one that chose to pass out literature instead of committing overt acts to get people to join. Both men had moved to Columbus within the past fifteen years from the South, one from Georgia, the other from Arkansas.

The top-ranking officer of the local chapter said many Columbus residents were anti-Klan due to what they had heard about the organization from years ago. He said his chapter would give food to the needy at Christmastime and also "do what we can to rid Columbus of interracial mixes, anything possible within the law and if we don't get caught outside the law. Now, I don't say we go out and kill anybody. I don't and we don't. I believe in peace and harmony for all."

The other Klansmen said the local chapter knew all the addresses of all interracial couples in Columbus. "But you won't see anything go in the paper about the Klan doing any violent acts on any of them," he said. "We are really peaceful. But on the other hand, should trouble arise and we are attacked in some way, we'd retaliate in a second."

A new wave of interest in the Klan here cropped up in May 1976, when the Columbus chapter purchased a small ad in the *Republic* each day for a week, seeking new members. The fact the ad was published struck a nerve with some residents.

It wasn't long before another local black man's yard was defiled with a cross, although both the victim and police said they couldn't be sure the Klan was actually responsible. A cross was found on the night of June 7 burning in the yard of Charles Rudy, a black man who lived in the 3200 block of Sycamore Street with his wife and children, all of whom were also black. Even though KKK literature was scattered on his lawn, Rudy figured the reason for the cross was that he was the only black foreman at Reliance Electric Company on Tenth Street.

Rudy had only lived in Columbus about eight months after moving here from Mississippi. He said he had been harassed at work due to his job as a supervisor. Klan literature and notes had been left on his desk, people falsely reported him to police for traffic violations and people used his name to order food and other items, he said. He also said he had asked for police escorts home from work three times following incidents at the plant.

Rudy said he expected the harassment at work, "but by involving my home and family, the persons responsible have overstepped their bounds." Rudy, who had witnessed Klan activity in Mississippi, said he thought the perpetrators were hiding behind the Klan.

A lodge for black people in the area was targeted at least three times in the fall of 1976, with the KKK implicated. Vandalism that cost thousands of dollars to repair was found on October 13 at the Golden Crown Lounge, at U.S. 31 and Base Line Road, southeast of the city.

In early March 1977, the Klan received permission from the Columbus Board of Works to hold a parade in the city on the afternoon of April 23. Early in April, the Klan revealed that members dressed in robes and security equipment would walk around the courthouse square, passing out literature. The news of a proposed march prompted some residents to ask the city to revoke the permit. But city officials said the plan as laid out by the Klan did not break any laws.

In response, Columbus North High School students organized their own march scheduled two hours earlier than the Klan's march. "Crusaders for Equality of All Americans" held its event at Mill Race Park, according to North seniors Garon Reeves and Mike Schafer, because "we don't want people to think the KKK is representative of the people of Columbus," Reeves said.

Neither march attracted much of a crowd on the cool, overcast day. The Klan's hour-long parade around the courthouse drew an estimated two hundred people, with few approaching the procession to get literature. The anti-Klan rally, meanwhile, was attended by about one hundred people, mostly students from North.

Klan members wore their robes and pointed hats but not masks. (By this time, few Klansmen kept their faces covered.) The student rally included speeches by its organizers as well as state senator Robert Garton, state representative Robert Hayes and the Reverend John R. Bean of North Christian Church.

Several of the anti-Klan protesters went to watch the Klan march and staged a "mini-march" behind the procession. There were scattered private debates between Klansmen and protesters, but there were no incidents.

Indiana Grand Dragon Jesse Jent was not happy with the anti-Klan crowd mixing in. "I call that deliberate agitation," he said. "That's what gets most of these guys fired up....Our people were instructed to keep their mouths shut and ignore it. If they [anti-Klan protesters] want to go out there and make a bunch of idiots of themselves, that's okay with me."

Mayor Andress, meanwhile, praised the students. "I was very pleased with the attitude and the principles this group of young people represent," he said. "If we're going to do away with racial prejudice and the feeling of inferior attitudes toward certain groups of people, the young people are going to do it."

While Klan news continued to come in from other parts of the country the rest of the decade, very little activity was seen in Bartholomew County, and the movement died out here.

5

LIKE FATHER, LIKE SON

BAD BOYS OF EARLY COLUMBUS

Theft, gambling and violence, often mixed with alcohol, were hallmarks of the McKinney and Bell brothers as they fashioned reputations as Columbus's worst sorts during the early history of the city. But not only were the brothers notorious bad guys, they were also part of multigenerational hoodlumism.

Joseph and John McKinney arrived on the scene prior to Bartholomew County's organization. They, and their three other brothers, came to the county from Wayne County, Virginia (now part of West Virginia), stopping at Laughery Creek, near present-day Rising Sun, Indiana, before moving to Columbus. Joseph served as sheriff in Laughery Creek and was the first sheriff and the second clerk in Bartholomew County. He was also the second man tried in a county court here. His brother John was also trouble. Their siblings, Lampkin, Thomas and Alfred, seemed to be more law-abiding.

Much of what we know of John and Joseph McKinney comes from a diary kept by General Harrison "Buck" Terrell and saved by noted local historian George Pence. Joseph and John raised racehorses, gambled and were part of the old Jockey Club, an organization of poor repute that regulated horse racing. They were also "two big, strong men with plenty of courage." They could also be quite gentlemanly when it suited them.

"With these qualities, they succeeded in supporting a reign of terror in the county for many years," according to historian Laura Long. "And then, as often happens with tyrants, there began to be opposition."

The first Johnson County Courthouse, used from 1821 to 1824. This was the courthouse where Sheriff Joseph McKinney was fined for assault in April 1821. *Bartholomew County Historical Society.*

Joseph McKinney helped organize the county and owned land north of Eleventh Street between what is now Washington Street and Indianapolis Road, where he ran a racetrack. He was also one of Columbus's early tavern keepers and obtained a license in 1827. He exuded plenty of personal charm and had some other admirable qualities. But he was also a bully, a heavy drinker and, at times, quite violent.

Those latter qualities got him into trouble often. During the first-ever session of the county court in April 1821, when he was the sheriff, he was fined for assault, with the judges recommending his fine be used to build roads. In October of that year, while still sheriff, McKinney was convicted of contempt of court and fined again. Later, as county clerk, he was tried for the embezzlement of more than $112 of county funds.

Fights among politicians were actually fairly common in the county's early history. Joseph McKinney was involved in perhaps the bloodiest one, when he was running for county clerk in 1828.

Newton C. Jones, a candidate for representative to the legislature, was the keeper of a Columbus tavern with his brother, Jack Jones. At Newton's house, Jack got into a dispute with Lampkin McKinney, known to most as Lamp. Jack Jones was accused of knocking Lamp down, although it was disputed exactly which Jones man did the deed.

Joseph McKinney heard a highly colorful account of the affair, at once proceeded to the Jones tavern and commenced berating Newton Jones, who was just about as powerful and courageous as his attacker and a skilled pugilist, too. It didn't take long for the men to start fighting, and soon, the floor, walls and ceiling were stained with blood.

They fought desperately for forty-five minutes and were not separated until they were so exhausted that they lay on the floor facing one another and occasionally striking out.

They were both elected to the offices for which they were candidates, but Jones died before the legislature assembled. It was thought by many that his death was due to the dreadful pounding he had suffered. He came out of the fight worse off than McKinney, who said years later he had received permanent injuries in the scrap.

Interestingly enough, shortly after his embezzling episode, McKinney won reelection as clerk over George E. Tingle, his assistant, who was considered quite principled. McKinney was none too pleased that his assistant was running for his office, and prior to the election, threatened Tingle, a fragile, modest and unassuming man. But Tingle let McKinney know any attack would be met with a counterattack, and with McKinney's embezzlement still fresh in voters' minds, McKinney backed down.

Not long before the election, the *Chronicle*, of which Lawson Duncan was editor, printed a scathing attack on the McKinneys, detailing immoralities and delinquencies with great severity. Some of the McKinneys visited Duncan and demanded to know who had authored the attacks. Duncan said he couldn't give the name of the author without asking the author for his approval, knowing full well if he didn't follow through, his head would most likely suffer some damage.

Duncan left word for the author, Williamson Terrell, cousin of General Terrell, to come to his office, but Duncan didn't say why. The next day, Williamson Terrell walked into town, wading through a river on the way, as he had no horse available. On the way to the newspaper office, he asked his cousin to go with him.

The two walked into the office, where Joseph McKinney and Duncan were waiting. Duncan explained that McKinney had taken offense to the article and demanded to know the name of the author.

"Do you mean the article signed 'Geoffrey?'" Terrell asked.

"Yes," answered Duncan.

"Then you can say that I am the author and that I hold myself responsible for all that it contains," Terrell said, before turning toward McKinney and adding, "And what are you going to do about it?"

Joseph McKinney decided not to do anything about it, which was probably a good idea on many fronts. He wound up getting reelected and remained in office until 1836, when he moved to Greensburg to open a tavern. He lived rather quietly there when he wasn't drinking.

During one drunken episode in Greensburg, Joseph attacked a tailor, who returned the attack by hitting him over the head with a cane, nearly killing him. McKinney, who had once saved a Bartholomew County man from drowning by rescuing him from the middle of a flooded stream, was never the same after the blow to his head. He moved to Oregon and drowned trying to cross a swollen stream.

Joseph's brother John came to Bartholomew County shortly after Joseph did. Together, they controlled the Democratic Party here for more than a decade. John, who was his brother's partner in all endeavors, both honest and dishonest, was more violent than Joseph, and he taught his sons to be that way, too.

John took over as sheriff in 1836, when John F. Jones resigned during two trials for which the penalty was hanging. "Jones couldn't make himself officiate at the hangings, but McKinney no doubt rather enjoyed himself," according to General Terrell.

Despite his dishonesty and immorality, McKinney was so entrenched in local politics that he remained sheriff until 1840. He then ran for the state legislature as a Democrat but was defeated by Williamson Terrell, the Whig candidate who had become a minister by this time.

For many years, John lived on a farm on Indianapolis Road adjoining the city. Later, he moved into a house on Jackson Street between Third and Fourth Streets, the location of the current post office.

Like his brother's, the story of John McKinney's death is also ironic. His neighbor across the alley on Jackson Street was a shoemaker named Cook. Both Cook and McKinney had several small children who used to get to quarreling. One day, McKinney decided he was going to spank one of the Cook children to teach him a lesson. He was just about to bring his hand down on the child's rear end when the Cooks's dog, "a savage beast," found its protective instincts.

The dog bit McKinney on the calf, forcing him to release the child. The injury should have been a minor one. But McKinney refused to have it treated. Over the course of a few days, the injury became a major one and put McKinney in bed. The leg became so swollen that amputation was advised. But McKinney refused, saying he preferred death to having his limb removed.

Just before he died, he sent for his former political rival and personal enemy, Williamson Terrell, and was baptized. He died at the age of forty-five. And while he may have repented of his sins at the end of his life and had many good qualities in addition to the less desirable ones, John McKinney left three sons who seemed to have missed out on the good qualities. At one point, they were all imprisoned simultaneously, two for murder and one for horse stealing.

The eldest of the three, Leander B. "Buck" McKinney, was the worst of the lot. General Terrell said of Buck, "He was in hot water from the beginning of life, and like the footman in the farce, he seems to have been born to bad luck. With his many excellent qualities—some that endeared him to his associates and schoolfellows so kindly that they speak kindly of him to this day and express sympathies for his sad fortunes, yet a disposition to drink changed him completely."

Buck learned the trade of rock throwing as a small boy and used it maliciously. "He threw a brickbat from his earliest boyhood with the skill with which an ancient Greek darted a javelin or as an Arabian swung a boomerang." One of Buck's earliest throws was through the window of Dr. Finley's office at the corner of Washington and Tipton (Third) Streets. The doctor picked up the stone, ran outside and nailed Buck in the back of the head with it, knocking him down.

Buck's stone throwing got him into trouble one time when a man from Kentucky named Williams was in town visiting the Jones tavern. Williams and another man were talking when Buck intruded. After getting annoyed by something Williams said, Buck struck the man with a concealed stone he carried around. Williams was knocked senseless, and when he recovered, he swore he would kill Buck. The Kentuckian never accomplished the task, though.

Buck did display some of his better behavior when he was in the military. He was a sergeant of Company F, Third Indiana Infantry, during the Mexican War, having enlisted in June 1846. He distinguished himself in the Battle of Buena Vista in Mexico before returning to Columbus after his discharge in 1847 immediately after the war.

But his criminal career blossomed shortly after he got home.

He was accused of stealing a horse from William Hayes in 1850, and although he was acquitted, many believed him guilty. Court records show he was arrested for assaulting a woman and charged with attempting to commit murder and official contempt. He managed to clear himself of these and many other charges in the next few months, but McKinney soon came to

Michael D. Emig was a close friend of Buck McKinney and helped him avoid a lynching, get paroled from prison and pardoned. *Bartholomew County Historical Society.*

be looked upon as a criminal of the worst class. One of his best friends and accomplices was Mike Emig, who got his friend out of a few scrapes.

In November 1857, Buck was walking along Washington Street with a boot under his arm when someone shot at him but missed. He was infuriated and would have killed the man had not Emig induced him to return home. But later, McKinney's wife asked him to go for a bucket of milk. As he walked uptown, saloonkeeper John Pettilott Sr. rushed from his establishment and fired at him. McKinney was not harmed, and he pursued his would-be murderer into the saloon. Jacob Rubrecht, a prominent man in town, tried to stop him. But McKinney, thinking he was about to be attacked, shot Rubrecht in the forehead, and the man died two days later.

After the shooting, McKinney secured the milk he had been sent for and calmly walked home. Officers followed him, but he would not give himself up for two hours, holding them at bay with a drawn revolver. Emig finally induced him to surrender, and McKinney was placed in jail. The murder created great excitement in Columbus, and nothing but the sight of McKinney dangling from a limb would appease some irate residents. A mob was organized to take him out of jail and hang him, and it would have done so had Emig not given a strong speech to them about letting the law take its course.

Another attempt at lynching McKinney would have followed had he not been taken to the jail at Madison without the public's knowledge. Buck escaped from that jail and committed a number of depredations before he was retaken. He was placed in jail again at Columbus and closely guarded every night, as it was known there were plans to lynch him.

It was shortly before the trial that something else occurred that greatly incensed the public against Buck. A new guard had been placed at the jail, and one night, seeing a man slipping by, the guard fired and killed him instantly. He thought the man was a member of a mob, but it turned out to be a friend of the sheriff's. McKinney was tried for murdering Rubrecht in April 1858 and found guilty in the first degree. His punishment was a great disappointment to many, as it was fixed at life imprisonment at Jeffersonville.

Although he was an orderly prisoner for the most part, McKinney added another murder to his list of crimes. He had always been noted for his cleanliness. One morning, after he had drawn a bucket of water, a convict who was especially dirty dropped a cup into the water and reached for it with a filthy hand. This so enraged McKinney that he struck the man several times with a knife, and the convict lived but a short time more. McKinney was not punished, as he was already under a life sentence.

After a few years in prison, he became trustworthy, and friends began a movement to get him pardoned. His old friend, Mike Emig, started a petition, and Governor Thomas A. Hendricks eventually signed the pardon, his last official act as governor before his term expired.

The move proved to be a mistake. After Buck returned to Columbus, he was constantly in trouble and nearly lost his life twice. John Miller shot him through the right arm in self-defense. And Buck's son whipped him nearly to death to protect his mother from Buck attacking her.

Left: The last official act Governor Thomas A. Hendricks performed in office was pardoning Buck McKinney. Hendricks was later vice president of the United States. *Library of Congress.*

Below: Buck McKinney was one of Columbus's most notorious criminals in the nineteenth century. *Courtesy of the* Republic.

NOTORIOUS BUCK M'KINNEY

LIES DEAD AT THE SOLDIERS' AND SAILORS' HOME AT MARION, IND.

Criminal Career Started In This City When He Was But a Youth—A Brave and Gallant Soldier.

Finally, Buck McKinney started wearing down from the rough life he had led, and friends secured him a place at the Soldiers Home at Dayton, Ohio. He was transferred to the Soldiers Home in Marion, Indiana, in 1890, and was in the hospital nearly all the time until his death three years later. Staff there kept him alive on alcoholic stimulants just about the entire time. His son made one visit, but Buck showed his dislike so plainly he never returned. Buck spent most of his pension buying presents for other soldiers.

While Buck might have been the worst of John McKinney's sons, he wasn't the only one who ran afoul of the law.

The next boy, John, was sentenced to prison for stealing horses. When he got out, he went to live peacefully in Rockford, just north of Seymour.

The youngest brother, Thomas, was nearly as bad as Buck. While quite young, he moved to Illinois, where he engaged in a life of crime, ending in his hanging. Tom McKinney led a gang of counterfeiters, successfully eluding authorities until he quarreled with a gang member over the division of spoils and murdered him in Vigo County, during a visit to Indiana. Tom buried the body and took off into Illinois again, settling about eight miles west of Vincennes with his mistress.

His sudden move across state lines left authorities suspicious, and they tracked him down. Faced with a lynching, he confessed his crime and told where the body of the missing man might be found. Tom was brought back to Vincennes, tried and convicted. His mother and father were at the execution, with the former sobbing and the latter saying sternly, "Tom, die like a man!"

The end of the McKinneys' run of lawlessness here nearly coincided with the rise of the Bell brothers.

The four sons of John W. Bell engaged in what was called a "reign of terror" in the city during the late 1880s and '90s. Nathan, Adolph, Alexander and Joseph Bell took turns terrorizing Columbus to varying degrees. They committed burglaries and assaults, stole horses and more.

For a time, John W. Bell owned a business dyeing fabric in Columbus. But "a fear of work and the earning of an honest living in early life is said to have led the old man to lay hands on property that did not belong to him; and his sons followed in his footsteps and have come to grief early in life," a story in the *Evening Republican* stated. He was once convicted of larceny.

Alex, the eldest son, was in trouble from the time he was very young; he was sent to the reformatory at Plainfield for the first time when he was but nine years old. He made several trips back there throughout his youth. While he was in Plainfield, he was an exemplary prisoner and became a "trusty," allowed the privileges of going about the grounds and running errands to town without surveillance. However, as good as he was in the reformatory, he was that bad outside of it.

"It seems that the bad blood was born and bred in him and all the good influence and kind treatment imaginable could not bring it out," the *Evening Republican* stated in February 1889.

One time, Alex was released from Plainfield on good behavior. Shortly thereafter, though, he disappeared from his home and stole some clothes. He returned the clothes but still couldn't be found. A month later, he stole clothes off someone else's line, got caught and was sent back to Plainfield. He was fifteen at the time.

In December 1888, he was charged with assault and battery on his sister and spent some time in jail. Less than two months later, he was arrested for robbing a store in Indianapolis, again taking clothing. Even his stepfather, Levi Cochrane of Columbus, was a victim of Alex's clothes-stealing habit.

As a nineteen-year-old, Alex received the maximum penalty of fourteen years for the Indianapolis store theft. The sentence was originally ten years, but the Bell lad mouthed off to Judge Nelson Keyes, saying he'd already served a term in a Tennessee prison, and if he had to go back to prison, he'd kill himself. Keyes then added four years to the sentence and sent him to the Jeffersonville prison. Alex's claim he'd served time in a Tennessee prison was fabricated. Nonetheless, it was generally agreed upon that he was already a hardened criminal by this time and deserved the maximum.

A few months later, Keyes amended the sentence to allow Alex out in seven years if he exhibited exemplary behavior while incarcerated. The prisoner promised to make a man of himself, adding that he had a hard life and had never had anyone train him properly. He did, in fact, make it out in seven years.

Nathaniel was probably involved in the most heinous crimes of the Bell boys.

Nat, as he was often called, sometimes went by the aliases Dick Jones and Dick McInnery. He decided one night to bust out several showroom windows in Columbus and steal from the stores. The robbery charges were dropped, and he pleaded guilty to the other charges, landing him a year in Jeffersonville. He was shot by a guard while trying to escape in March 1889. The wound was originally thought to be fatal, but Nat survived. When he was released, Nat continued his life of crime.

On Thanksgiving night 1889, Nathan, about twenty-seven years old, blew up the safe of grain and coal merchant Len Griffith at Fifth and Franklin Streets with the help of William Watson. The pair took $280 in cash. Nathan skipped town and couldn't be located for nearly a year. He finally came back to Columbus and took a job at Crump's brickyard. Soon, he was arrested and charged with the crime. When Nathan showed up in the circuit court in Columbus in October 1890, he saw two familiar faces there to testify in his trial. One was a prisoner from Michigan City and the other a prisoner from Jeffersonville.

Watson was the one from the southern prison, having already been sentenced; the other was Nathan's father, who was serving time up north for larceny, the same crime his son was facing. When father and son first met in court, they didn't recognize one another. Soon after realizing who Nathan was, John W. was said to have buried his head in his hands. "The pains of remorse must have struck deep in the heart of the old man," an *Evening Republican* report said, "as he viewed his son a prisoner at the bar, to whom he should have set a better example earlier in life."

The safe incident led to Nathan's third trip to Jeffersonville, this time with a seven-year sentence. But he got the itch to run again and escaped with three others in May 1893. The four dug out into the prison yard, creating a tunnel two feet underground that was ten feet long and two feet in diameter. They worked for months on their creation, using knives to cut away at the earth and carrying the dirt away in their hands. Nathan Bell wasn't heard from again.

The Bell boys were fairly quiet around Columbus for a couple of years in the early 1890s, perhaps due to the fact most of them had been incarcerated. But they made headlines again in July 1894, when three of them were involved in a fight at the Belvedere Hotel, on the northwest corner of Third and Franklin. Adolph had recently gotten back to town from the house of correction, and Alex returned from the southern prison. Joseph had managed to stay out of prison, while Nathan was still apparently on the lam, and their father's whereabouts were unknown. John W. Bell disappeared after being released from Michigan City.

On the morning of July 27, the family reunion turned ugly. An argument between Joseph and Adolph erupted over a business arrangement whereby they were planning to sell a certain kind of pants stretcher. The two came to blows. Alex tried to play the part of peacemaker, which Adolph did not take to kindly. Adolph drew a razor and left a two-inch-long, half-inch-deep gash under Alex's left ear. Alex grabbed a chair and smashed it over Adolph's head, knocking him down.

City marshal George Lewellen showed up and took Adolph to the county jail. Alex had his wound dressed and was soon back at the hotel talking

The Bell brothers engaged in a bloody fight among themselves at the Belvedere Hotel in 1894. *Bartholomew County Historical Society.*

about the incident. Adolph, who had worked at the hotel, was charged with assault and battery with the intent to commit murder.

While awaiting trial, Adolph got himself sent to the county jail's version of solitary confinement, a dark room below the main jail floor. He had been roughing up multiple prisoners and was one of several prisoners who had broken iron bars out of the windows and hidden them in their cells. He was found guilty and sentenced to six months in jail.

Alex was fined and sent to jail for intoxication in October 1895. One month later, he was back in jail for kicking in the door of Louis Buchman while drunk. For his efforts, Alex received twenty days in jail.

Alex was at it again in 1896, stealing two horse-and-buggy combos, one in Columbus and one in Greenwood. He was apprehended in July in Brown County and put into the Bartholomew County jail. While awaiting trial, he and another inmate, Simeon Bryant, threw the jailer to the ground as he picked up dishes from their lunch. The two men ran out of the jail and escaped. There were no other authorities at the jail at that time, and the pair made it out of sight rather easily.

Authorities tracked down Bell and Bryant in Brown County, although the two managed to fool a pack of bloodhounds first. They stole a mule and rode it for a good portion. But one of the men would get off and walk every once in a while, allowing the dogs to keep picking up the trail. The fugitives then stole a horse and buggy south of Columbus, making it impossible for the dogs to follow the trail.

Authorities decided to look for Bell and Bryant at the home of Bell's father-in-law near Storyville, about eighteen miles west of Columbus, and they found Bell there. When captured, a letter Bell had written to Sheriff Vincent Thompson was found in his valise, stating the sheriff would never see him again.

Back in jail, Alex made plans to escape again. He wrote a letter to his wife, intending for her to meet him in Indianapolis after his next escape. The letter was found on an inmate who was being released from jail a week or so after Bell had been recaptured. The sheriff also found a razor in Bell's cell that had been fashioned into a saw, costing Bell his visitation privileges.

Bell's constant attempts to escape continued, the next time with him "acting like a crazy man at two in the morning, frightening the other prisoners," the *Evening Republican* said. When the sheriff went upstairs to see what all the noise was about, Bryant, the prisoner who had escaped with Bell the previous time, handed the sheriff a saw that Bell had used to cut a hole in the floor and saw off the two inside bars in one window. The iron lattice work outside the window was all that was keeping Bell from freedom, but getting through that would have taken all night.

The sheriff later found out how Alex had managed to obtain the saws. He had made a crude bow and arrow with a stave from a barrel and some string and shot it out into the street. One of his brothers attached the saws to the string, and Alex reeled them in.

Alex was quite depressed over this failed escape attempt and voluntarily handed over another saw he had hidden. However, it didn't stop him from causing problems in jail.

A few weeks later, he and Bryant started a fire in their cell in an attempt to get out. Inmates would occasionally light their beds on fire if they were not happy with their treatment or if they just wanted to cause a stir. Bell and Bryant had been doing this for two or three mornings straight when, on the morning of September 25, 1896, they took it to an extreme.

Both set their beds aflame in different areas of the upper cells. Bell's bed became virtually engulfed and was held up to a ventilator that led to the jail hospital, which made the iron sheeting red-hot and set the hospital floor on fire. The fire spread to the roof and burned for an hour and a half before being extinguished. Smoke was noticed early on, but locals figured it was just another routine bed burning and paid little mind until the smoke got pervasive. The blaze caused an estimated $20,000 damage. (The building was only estimated to be worth $36,000, and it was not covered by insurance.)

The fourth building used as the Bartholomew County Jail, built in 1870, was on the courthouse square. It suffered significant fire damage in 1896 when Alex Bell and another inmate set fire to their beds. *Bartholomew County Historical Society.*

The ploy didn't work, as a handcuffed Bell and Bryant, along with the one other prisoner there at the time, were taken away to be housed elsewhere.

If all of Alex Bell's hijinks before this had not agitated the citizens here, this one infuriated them. "He is a bad man and the sooner society is relieved of such a man the better it will be for this community," the *Evening Republican* stated.

By the end of the month, Bell and Bryant had pleaded guilty to grand larceny from stealing the horse, with Judge Thomas F. Hord sentencing them both to ten years in Jeffersonville. Bell felt lucky not to get the maximum of fourteen years.

This sentence signaled the end of the Bells' reign of terror here.

Alex was never heard from again around Columbus. Adolph and his wife moved to Chicago right about this time. Joseph was paroled by Governor James A. Mount in July 1897 from a fifteen-month sentence. He spent the next few years in Columbus before moving to Indianapolis.

6

THE BUSINESS OF SELLING SEX

While the prostitution business has been going on since ancient times, the trade has generally been illegal and frowned upon in the United States. There have been periods, though, when the practice has either been looked at as a necessary evil or allowed to exist while authorities looked the other way.

Reports of houses of ill repute in Columbus have been made since well before the start of the twentieth century. A woman on Mulberry Street (now First Street) was accused of keeping a house of ill fame in August 1872. Hideous noises were heard coming from the house seven times a week. The lady's explanation? Cats.

But it wasn't until the late 1870s that the city featured more than a smattering of these types of houses. The arrest of two women on July 31, 1877, confirmed that supposition. City Marshal Ben F. Fewell arrested Miranda Dowell and Phebe Workman, "two unmitigated prostitutes," for running a house of prostitution, and the women were assessed a twenty-five-dollar fine, plus court costs.

A story in the *Evening Republican* reported:

> *Their den has borne a most blemished reputation for a year or more, and is an eyesore and object of disgust to all respectable people. But now that the birds are caged, and if the honor and virtue of the city is to be maintained, keep them there, and put with them the many others here whom a decent man or woman would blush to meet face to face. This has gone far enough....*

We hope our officers may keep it up until every den of prostitution is broken up, their inmates [prostitutes] dealt with to the severest and fullest extent of the law, and our beautiful little city stands upon the pedestal of virtue and morality.

The problem only got worse, though.

Several arrests were made over the next four years or so in connection with houses of ill fame. Many times, these houses were in one of the city's slum areas. Occasionally, the illegal activity was held elsewhere.

In July 1880, police ventured into the woods near Crump's brickyard by the White River to break up a gang that for several days had lived there "in a most licentious manner." There were two men, one woman and two girls, ages sixteen and thirteen, living in two dilapidated tents. The girls had been put up as prostitutes and were visited by several young men and boys. "The acts of the men and the women show them to be of the most degrading type and their acts bestial in the full sense of the word," the *Evening Republican* reported. "The officers have done well in driving from this vicinity such creatures, especially the older ones who are deserving of a coat of tar and feathers."

The *Republican*, on February 10, 1881, wondered why only the women were getting arrested when there was a police raid on a brothel. "If a few of them [men] were brought into court, publicly exposed and punished, it might have quite as good effect as to punish the poor dissolute women."

The story of how two Columbus girls had been lured into a life of prostitution was told in the *Republican* in October 1881. The friends, ages eighteen and sixteen, began flirting about a year earlier with two strangers who said they were travelers from Cincinnati. The flirting turned physical, and it was said the strangers found the girls to be "young, giddy and thoughtless creatures."

The men's trips to Columbus became more frequent, and they stayed longer each time. When they came to town, they brought small presents for the girls, who were flattered to the point of allowing the men to gain their confidence. The girls were soon convinced to give up their virginity and told not to tell anyone of these activities. They eventually moved to a distant city to enter lives of prostitution.

Another young girl who got involved with prostitution here was said to be quite a "sad case." Mattie Ferguson, seventeen or eighteen years old, had already been arrested several times when she was found in August 1882 "entertaining a group of males ages 14 to 20" in an old icehouse by the toll bridge just west of the river near the intersection of what is now State Roads 46 and 11. She showed up in court to face charges of prostitution bareheaded, barefooted and wearing a man's coat. She paid a fine and spent sixty days in jail. The *Republican* expressed wishes that there were a reformatory she could go to instead of jail, as her stints in lockup had not helped.

Ella Bishop, one of the most notorious prostitutes in Columbus before 1900, was sent to jail a few times, "without changing countenance." But when she was sent to jail in March 1884, she finally broke down and sobbed like a child. Both Bishop and Jennie Cooper had been charged with prostitution after plying their trade on Sunday evenings in a railroad boxcar. It was said that the night was so dark and the boxcars so numerous on the night of the raid that the males consorting with them were able to get away undetected.

Throughout this period, the city government came under fire for averting its eyes when it came to vice in the city. In addition to the city being in debt and taxes being high, the *Evening Republican* wrote on October 18, 1884, that "no attempt is made to enforce many of the laws. Saloons, gambling hells and houses of prostitution are open night and day the year round and are never molested, although the law is violated hundreds of times every week. Where there are any prosecutions they are a mockery of justice and instituted simply to put money into the pockets of the officers."

Despite these pleas, the practice of prostitution continued nearly unabated for some time.

Catharine Dunlap was found guilty of keeping a house of ill fame in June 1885. A month later, she was involved in quite a flap. William Bradford, who when sober was a fine gentleman, came to her house on Pearl Street drunk one Saturday night. He was followed by his wife, who suspected him of being up to no good since he hadn't given her any money for expenses that day as was his custom, and he said something strange that morning. Mrs. Bradford knocked on the door of the brothel and asked that her husband come home with her immediately. Mr. Bradford slipped out through the garden gate and headed for home, while his wife was beaten badly with broomsticks by Dunlap and her daughter, both of whom faced assault and battery charges. Mr. Bradford was found guilty of visiting a house of ill fame.

Dunlap once again found herself facing charges of running a house of ill fame the following February. She was told to leave the city, which she did for a time, but she came back and got herself into an even bigger mess six years later, when a raid on her Pearl Street house revealed that she was harboring "two of Shelbyville's fast women." City Marshal George Lewellen had had his eye on the house for two weeks because it had become quite annoying to her neighbors to get gentlemen callers at the wrong address in the middle of the night.

Sometimes, when men did get charged with visiting a brothel, the madam came to his rescue. Michael Adams found that to be the case in 1885, as his fine was partially paid for by the woman in charge of the house he visited.

The sex trade in Columbus seemed to ease off for a few years, as city officials stepped up efforts to put houses of ill fame out of business. There were still occasional arrests, most notably on Smoky Row. But things were fairly quiet on the prostitution front until the 1890s brought another wave of it.

Jane Hornback and Alice Sullivan were considered two of the most notorious women in Columbus in the early 1890s. Hornback, in fact, was charged with inducing her niece into prostitution. By 1900, citizens reported that four houses of ill repute were associated with saloons in the city.

But the most famous madam of them all was Lillian "Todie" Tull. She began operating brothels in Columbus in the mid-1890s and spent roughly twenty years in the business here. Her houses were at Fourth and Sycamore Streets, Sixth and Wilson Streets, Union and Second Streets, 538 North Jackson Street, just south of the Pennsylvania Railroad Depot, and finally 910 North Jackson.

Todie's houses were raided rather frequently, but perhaps not as frequently as some others around town, as she tried to keep alcohol and violence at bay. There were several interesting incidents at Tull's houses, though.

A house she ran was vandalized "in the name of morality" on the night of December 1, 1894. She was only eighteen years old and already considered a lewd woman in Columbus when her house was stoned and clubbed. And while sentiment ran against the type of business she conducted, sentiment ran even deeper against the vandals. "That there has been too much latitude given the lewd woman there can be no doubt," a story in the *Republican* stated. "But at the same time a remedy for this evil should never be encouraged that is greater under the law than the evil itself."

Even so, the vandalism achieved its goal. Alerted by the crime, police raided the house, finding three men and three women there. Tull and the other women faced prostitution charges. One of the men, William Holman, said he was just delivering a late lunch to the house. His excuse didn't fool the judge, who fined him for visiting a house of ill fame.

About six months later, Tull and two Indianapolis women were arrested after a raid of her house. Tull refused to go with police, sitting on the floor until she was forcibly moved into a carriage for a ride to jail.

ACE FOSTER SHOT BY LILLIAN TULL

YOUTH TR ED TO GAIN AD-MITTANCE TO RESORT—SERIOUS RESULTS.

SIXTEEN AFFIDAVITS FILED

Police Court Full This Morning —All Enter Pleas of Not Guilty And Will Be Tried Later— Were All Re-leased on Bond.

Notorious madam Lillian "Todie" Tull shot Asa "Ace" Foster when he tried to break down the door of her house of ill repute in 1903. *Courtesy of the* Republic.

Tull eventually purchased a seventeen-room, two-story brick house at what now would be the northwest corner of Ninth and Jackson Streets for $1,950. She spent another $3,000 to $5,000 to furnish it quite lavishly, especially the bedding. The building, which had housed a school called the Bartholomew

County Academy, predating Columbus High School, became Tull's Wayside Inn, where she plied her trade for the next dozen years or so.

One of the major stories coming from a Tull house was the 1903 shooting of a boy who would not accept *No* for an answer. In the early morning of December 18, five drunk boys went to her place and asked to be allowed to enter. This request was denied, which didn't sit well with them. The boys beat on one of the doors, then threw a beer bottle against it.

After carousing a while, the boys went to another door of the house, where they once again demanded admittance. Tull ordered them to go away, but Asa "Ace" Foster ripped the screen and kicked the door down. Tull drew a .38 revolver and shot four times, with one bullet hitting Foster in the mouth, tearing through his palate and lodging in his neck. Foster was taken to the Commercial Hotel and then to his home on Brown Street, where he fell under the care of Dr. A.J. Banker.

Tull's house wasn't the first one the boys tried to enter that night. Prior to their escapade there, they tried to get into another house of ill repute, also on North Jackson Street. This one was run by Maria Wadsworth, better known as "Old Rye." A similar scenario played out there, with the boys trying to break down the door and the owner pulling out a revolver and shooting. That time, nobody got hit. In fact, one of the boys grabbed the revolver and kept it.

The boys were charged with assault. Both Tull and Wadsworth were charged with keeping a house of prostitution, and the women in their houses were charged with being prostitutes. Tull also faced a charge of assault and battery with the intent to commit murder. Foster recovered and pleaded guilty to his charges.

It wasn't the only time drunken mobs tried to enter local houses of prostitution in those days. A group of men from Brown County made the trip east to Columbus in August 1903 with the intent "to paint the town any color that suited." After trying to gain entrance to a house of ill repute, they chased after a young man who had been camping on the riverbank and beat him with clubs.

Tull was never one to back down from anyone, as the Ace Foster shooting might have indicated. In March 1907, she accused two of the women who had made homes in her 910 North Jackson Street house of stealing nearly $100 worth of clothing. The women, Estie Seth and Ruth Barnett, alias Georgia Janway, fled to Indianapolis. Bartholomew County sheriff Irwin A. Cox found the women but was not allowed to bring them to Columbus to face grand larceny charges yet, as they were in the process of facing other charges there. When they showed up for their court hearing in April, they

TWO WOMEN CHARGED WITH GRAND LARCENY

Lillian Tull Files Affidavits in Justice Stader's Court Against Two Former Sojourners.

An affidavit has been filed in Justice Stader's court against Estie Seth and Ruth Barnett, alias Georgia Janway, who until recently made their homes with Lillian Tull on north Jackson street, charging them with grand larceny.

Two alleged prostitutes, Estie Seth and Ruth Barnett, were charged with grand larceny in 1907. *Courtesy of the* Republic.

were accompanied by an elderly woman "who was much be-decked with diamonds" as well as a "colored maid," a story in the *Evening Republican* said. The women pleaded guilty to petit larceny, were fined about twenty dollars (which was paid by the woman who accompanied them) and went to jail for twenty-four hours.

Seth and Barnett then filed affidavits against Tull for something that was never made clear. But when the women found out they would have to pay their own way to Columbus to prosecute the cases, they changed their minds and refused to sign.

Tull was sued in July 1907 for not making payments on an electric player-piano that she had in her place of business. The piano had a slot on the side, so that when patrons dropped a nickel or dime into it, the piano would play. The instrument was valued at $650, and Fuller & Currens, which had sold it to her, sought $350 in damages. Tull ended up getting to keep the piano.

While Tull avoided some of the other issues that prompted raids on houses of ill repute, hers wasn't immune to them. And with increasing pressure from the recently organized Civil League, authorities started cracking down harder on her type of business.

Tull's house was paid a visit by the Civic League, Captain George Smitha of the night police force and Sheriff Cox about 11:30 p.m. on October 26, 1907. The raid resulted in the arrests of nine men and five women and the confiscation of 204 bottles of Champagne Velvet beer that had been stowed in a buggy. In addition to the charges of running a house of prostitution, she also faced charges of operating a blind tiger, as she was selling beer without a license.

Since the reorganization of the Civic League in Columbus four years earlier, considerable attention had been paid to the illegal sale of beer and liquor. One of the stated goals of the league was to put Todie Tull out of business. The madam had unwittingly tipped off the Civic League a few days before the raid by sending out picture postcards advertising reduced rates at her establishment. "The nerve of this almost took the breath from some of the reformers, and they decided to get busy at once," the *Republican* said.

Judge O.P. Turner and prosecuting attorney Albert W. Phillips were told that the raid would be coming and that they should be ready early Sunday morning to do some work, while Cox and Smitha obtained a search warrant ahead of time. On the night of the raid, Cox and Smitha pulled the bell at the front door, and when the landlady answered, they barged in. The other members of the raiding party waited outside to nab anyone who tried to escape.

During the raid, a group of young men sought admittance to the house. When a police officer answered the door, they scurried as fast as they could.

About two o'clock in the morning, authorities marched the fourteen who had been apprehended down Washington Street to see Justice Turner. All the men pleaded guilty and were fined. Tull pleaded not guilty. One of the other women pleaded guilty to living in a house of ill repute, while the other three pleaded not guilty. One of the men was rumored to be Tull's husband. Conviction of running a blind tiger carried a fine of between $50 and $500, plus a jail sentence of between thirty days and six months.

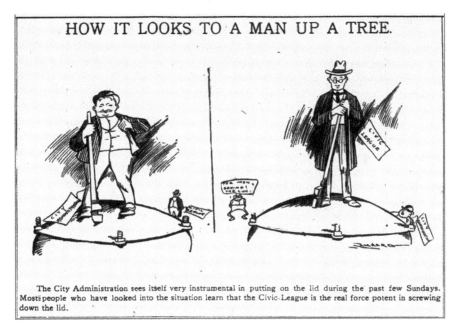

HOW IT LOOKS TO A MAN UP A TREE.

The City Administration sees itself very instrumental in putting on the lid during the past few Sundays. Most people who have looked into the situation learn that the Civic-League is the real force potent in screwing down the lid.

An editorial carton by Louis Richards in 1907 shines light on the job the recently organized Civic League was doing to help the city get rid of prostitution and those who broke booze laws. *Courtesy of the* Republic.

When Sheriff Cox went back to the house to get the beer, he hitched his horse up to the buggy, but there was no room for a driver, the vehicle being so full of beer. So he walked his horse to the jail, with other members of the raiding party walking alongside, looking like pallbearers. The beer was stored at the jail until after the trial.

The raid was not wholly supported by city officials. One of the women who was arrested said that she knew the administration of Mayor James Cochrane and Marshal Ed Horton didn't order the raid and claimed it had actually offered the house protection. A few days after the raid, some anti–Civic Leaguers were pushing to have Smitha removed from his duties because of his role. Horton was reportedly upset that the raid took place without his knowledge and said he would resign if Smitha were not fired. Smitha, however, was praised by others for doing his duty.

A conversation held between some police officers and Perry Wooden, president of the Civic League, showed the thinking on the organization's stance on prostitution and illegal booze sales at that time. Policeman Frank Huffman asked Wooden if the Civic League simply wanted to stop the sale of illegal booze in these types of houses or if the organization wanted to put the brothels out of business altogether. Wooden and attorney William H. Everroad informed the officer that they wanted to rid Columbus of these houses altogether, which would solve the problem of liquor being sold there.

The Civic League meant business and aimed to aid police in any way possible to clean up prostitution and illegal booze sales in the city. Another well-known brothel had closed recently and planned to stay out of business until this reform wave spent itself.

When Lillian Tull's trial came up at Walesboro on November 22, it was the first case under the new blind tiger laws to be tried in local courts. She agreed to plead guilty on all charges and was fined. And all three of her employees pleaded guilty to their charges, too. Tull got off cheaper than she might have otherwise because she signed an agreement not to break the blind tiger or prostitution laws anymore. She also lost 204 bottles of beer, valued at a dime a bottle. Cox poured out the twenty-five and a half gallons of suds into the jail yard a week later to comply with state law.

The *Evening Republican* declared that Lillian Tull's resort was no more and she was moving. "This final chapter ends the Tull raid. The woman has paid her fines and left the city and all of the beer is now making itself feel at home in the White River."

While Todie Tull did indeed leave Columbus, she didn't leave the brothel business. In October 1908, she was in an Indianapolis court after being accused of luring a sixteen-year-old girl into being a prostitute at a house of ill repute there.

The former Wayside Inn at 910 North Jackson that Tull still owned was the victim of an apparent arson on the night of August 23, 1909. Coal oil was found throughout the house, and an empty whiskey bottle was found near the front door. The woman who lived there with her son noticed the fire, and both got out unharmed. It was said that people had been trying to enter the home for some time prior to the fire.

The damage to the house itself wasn't bad, except for smoke and water, but the bedding and furnishings suffered a great deal of damage. In fact, there was fire in each room of the house, most of which were started in mattresses or couches. A small building out back, in which a lighting plant for the house was located, was completely destroyed.

Shortly after the fire, Tull put her house up for sale in an auction, and Charles Lambert bought it for $4,000. But as with just about any event in Tull's adult life, this transaction wasn't without controversy. She later sued Lambert, accusing him of not making any payments, and demanded the deed back. In June 1911, she was awarded the house.

It wasn't long before Tull, now thirty-five years old, was back to her old ways in Columbus. This time, she had a partner.

In September 1911, Tull and another madam who shared the house and workload, Nettie Henderson Boullie, were implicated in white slavery by a Fort Wayne newspaper. The women had attempted to entice a seventeen-year-old girl to come to Columbus from Fort Wayne with the promise of a job. The local women were aided by Clifford Grove, proprietor of a soft drink establishment at Seventh and Jackson who had sent a letter to Sadie Holley suggesting he'd enjoy meeting her when she arrived here.

Holley had originally heard of the promise of a job in Columbus when she was living in Michigan City. A vagrant by the name of Jesse "One Leg" Dobson, who was staying at the boardinghouse where Holley lived, told the girl that he knew a woman in Columbus who could offer her a job and a way out of the miserable life she was leading. Dobson was a former Columbus resident who had his leg amputated below the knee many years prior after a large wheel crushed his ankle. He also worked with Grove for a time here.

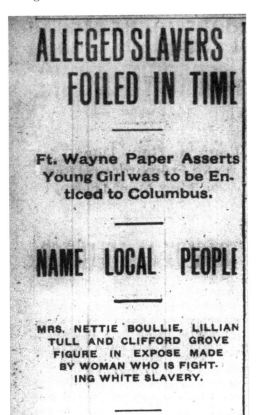

ALLEGED SLAVERS FOILED IN TIME

Ft. Wayne Paper Asserts Young Girl was to be Enticed to Columbus.

NAME LOCAL PEOPLE

MRS. NETTIE BOULLIE, LILLIAN TULL AND CLIFFORD GROVE FIGURE IN EXPOSE MADE BY WOMAN WHO IS FIGHTING WHITE SLAVERY.

Holley started corresponding with Boullie, and the letters continued after Holley and her mother moved to Fort Wayne. In her letters to the girl, Boullie painted a picture of a woman in poor health needing a girl to take care of her and said she just couldn't find anyone near Columbus who could do the job. Holley was sent a railroad ticket to come to Columbus, but she was persuaded to stay home.

The girl then ran into Katherine Fiske, who was

Because the girl refused their invitation, well-known madams Lillian Tull and Nettie Henderson Boullie were not charged with engaging in white slavery in 1911, although they had been accused of attempting to lure a Fort Wayne girl here for the purposes of forcing her to become a prostitute. *Courtesy of the* Republic.

lecturing in Fort Wayne about white slavery, and gave Boullie's letters to Fiske. The lecturer called the Columbus police and asked them to break up what she called a white slave ring. Boullie and Tull claimed they did not contact the girl with immoral purposes in mind. Since the girl never left Fort Wayne, police there said no laws had been broken in Allen County. Tull and Boullie never faced charges here either.

Another similar case cropped up in Columbus later that month when two girls from Seymour, ages nineteen and fifteen, came here and stayed for two nights at the Jackson Street home of Ella Gibson. The woman told the girls that she would get them jobs at the best hotel in the city to lure them here. But when they arrived, she took them to the Tull house; the girls refused to stay. Gibson reiterated that the girls needed to go to the Tull house and spoke to them of a life of lavish luxury.

The girls were sent to lodge with two men at the Western Hotel at the corner of Second and Washington. The men gave false names when checking in and registered as being with their wives. The father of the younger girl saw them in the city a day or so later, grabbed them and went to the police. One of the men, William Pope, was charged with encouraging acts of child delinquency and Gibson with contributing to the delinquency of a child.

Tull's house, which she had been trying to pass off as a boardinghouse, was raided again in December 1912, with one man and four women getting charged. Tull, who was in Louisville at the time, was indignant upon her return after finding out everyone pleaded guilty. She pleaded not guilty to running a house of prostitution. But when the trial came around, she changed her plea to guilty after seeing the evidence amassed against her.

The city government had recently employed officials to keep track of all houses of ill repute. All women who worked in the Tull house were asked to register, ensuring that they were there of their own free will and there was no white slaving going on there. The registration records were taken as proof that the house had been a place of prostitution.

About a week after getting fined again, Tull announced that she was closing the only registered disorderly house in the city and leaving Columbus. This time, finally, that was probably true.

In mid-April, the Tull house was in the limelight once again. She had leased the house to an Indianapolis woman, Catherine White, who was running it as a brothel. It was found out as such when Lewis Cross went to police and said he'd been attacked by a man and woman at the house and robbed of a gold watch and fifty dollars cash that had been cut out of a pocket of his coat. When questioned later, Cross admitted that he had not been robbed; he cut his own coat and only told the story for effect. Everyone involved in the house got fined, which White paid, but Cross also got fifteen days of hard labor on the rock pile for lying to police.

In October 1913, Lillian Tull Taylor, as she was listed, and a man listed as her husband sold the house, Lot 22 in Doup Addition, to Francis T. Crump for $100.

Prostitution in Columbus certainly did not end with Lillian "Todie" Tull leaving town. The mid-1920s saw another slight boom in the trade, and again in the early 1940s. But the days of the acceptance of such houses as Todie ran fell further out of favor in the city.

7

THE PRINCE OF RASCALS

*N*obody knew how William Henry Schreiber could afford the life of luxury he was living in Columbus in the late 1880s. The twenty-two-year-old teller and bookkeeper at First National Bank was earning a modest sixty-two dollars per month in 1888.

Yet he lived much richer.

Schreiber lived in an elegant, two-room suite above a laundry in the Crump building on Fourth Street. The apartment was lavishly furnished, with fine, upholstered furniture and a brass bedstead with rich coverings. His two rooms were connected by an arch, under which hung silk curtains. In one of the rooms sat a billiard table, dumbbells, boxing gloves and wine cases.

Schreiber dressed in the finest clothes available, purchasing a new suit nearly every month at a cost of seventy-five to ninety dollars each. His cigar bill averaged a dollar a day, and he had recently begun eating ten dollars' worth of oysters per week, delivered to his room from Burnett's Restaurant, 435 Washington Street.

He had purchased two racehorses and was becoming quite the ladies' man. In fact, he had presented a lady friend with a diamond ring appraised at $150. Schreiber was also known to wear valuable diamonds himself.

There was one particular woman whom Schrieber had been keeping in royal style. He had sent large amounts of money to a woman thought to be named Fannie Carr James, of Chicago. She had visited Schreiber the previous summer, registering at the St. Denis Hotel, 436 Washington Street,

First National Bank, founded by the Crump family, was located at Fourth and Washington Streets from 1882 to 1987. The building now houses a PNC branch. *Bartholomew County Historical Society.*

as Florence Carr. She was about eighteen years old and quite attractive. After leaving Columbus, she got ill and stayed in Indianapolis for a time, during which Schreiber visited her often.

These instances, it was noted, were only some of the extravagant purchases Schreiber had made. By all appearances, he seemed to be a wealthy man, which made many of his acquaintances wonder where all his money came from.

It certainly didn't come from his father, August Schreiber, a German immigrant who moved to Columbus from Bavaria in 1843. August owned a small brewery and saloon in the city and was not rich by any means.

Will was born in Columbus and had been with First National Bank for six years by the time he started spending wildly beyond his apparent means. He started as a teller when he was sixteen years old, and after two years, he took over as bookkeeper when Jake Harris resigned.

Schreiber's need for extravagance ate away at him until it culminated in his robbing his own employer. On the night before Thanksgiving 1888, November 28, Schreiber ripped off First National Bank at the southeast corner of Fourth and Washington Streets and skipped town.

The day of the robbery, Schreiber put some personal papers in the supposedly burglar-proof safe, where the money was kept. Just before closing, he asked to retrieve his papers. He did, but he also took $8,500 in cash (well over $200,000 in today's dollars) and $300,000 in nonnegotiable securities from the safe, walked out of the safe into the vault area, dropped the cash and notes on the floor and kicked them under some furniture without anyone noticing.

A moment later, the time lock clicked on the safe, and it would not open again until Friday morning, the day after the holiday. Shortly after that, the vault door was closed and locked, too.

Schreiber was in the habit of going into the bank after hours to work on the books, which were kept in the vault. And having been a respected employee for so long, he had been given the combination to the lock on the vault door. When he returned later that night, he opened the vault door and grabbed the money that he had kicked out of sight earlier.

He stuffed everything into a valise he had brought with him and left the bank. The securities would actually do Schreiber no good, but having them replaced would cause the bank some big headaches.

Having previously told his employers that he had planned to go to Indianapolis for Thanksgiving, Schreiber's departure on the ten o'clock train heading north caused no suspicion. But instead of staying in Indianapolis, he got on another train there and proceeded on a circuitous route to Toronto.

When Lewis "L.K." Ong, the cashier, and Captain William J. Lucas, president of the bank, opened the safe at the start of business Friday morning, they noticed the money was missing. When Schreiber didn't show up for work at his scheduled time, he was suspected of the theft. About 10 o'clock, Ong and Lucas's fears were confirmed when they received a telegram from Schreiber.

It said: "I arrived here this morning. Will be at Queen's Hotel, Toronto, Saturday morning. Schreiber."

Where exactly Schreiber had arrived was not mentioned. And it was not known why he had sent the telegram. Was it to throw police off his track? Was he not really going to Canada? Or was he taunting his employer that he got away with it?

Above: John S. Crump sits inside the vault he purchased to put into the First National Bank. Note the safe in the background. *Bartholomew County Historical Society*.

Right: Bookkeeper Will Schreiber robbed his employer, First National Bank, on the night before Thanksgiving in 1888. The headline erroneously states that Schreiber was a teller at the time of the robbery. *Courtesy of the* Republic.

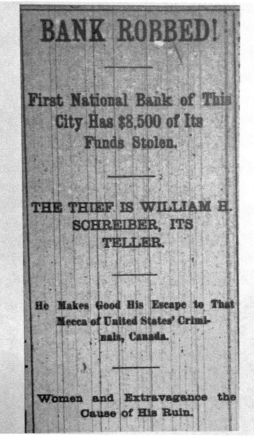

BANK ROBBED!

First National Bank of This City Has $8,500 of Its Funds Stolen.

THE THIEF IS WILLIAM H. SCHREIBER, ITS TELLER.

He Makes Good His Escape to That Mecca of United States' Criminals, Canada.

Women and Extravagance the Cause of His Ruin.

Soon, authorities had another Canada connection. It was learned that before Schreiber had left Columbus, he'd received a telegram from his lady friend in Chicago that read "I leave for Canada tonight. The funds are all O.K." It was signed "F.C. James," causing her to be considered an accessory to the theft.

The robbery didn't threaten the bank's solvency. There was plenty of cash on hand, and its capital stock was $100,000. However, when the news leaked out about the robbery late Friday, many depositors demanded their money on Saturday. There was no worry, however, that this run would be big enough to cause First National to be unable to pay investors their dividends.

If and when Schreiber were to be extradited to the United States, a possibility since Canada and the United States had an agreement in place for such crimes as this, he would be charged with grand larceny.

The robbery fueled many rumors, one of which was that Schreiber had absconded with $10,000 in government bonds. Some Columbus residents suggested that he had been altering his books, enabling him to live his lavish lifestyle. Neither of these allegations proved to be true.

Many blamed bank officials for continuing to employ a man whose extravagant spending habits were well known. But those who employed him were not aware of the extent of Schreiber's lifestyle. Ong, who worked closely with him, said he only knew of the racehorse purchases and was not aware of any of the man's other elegant lifestyle choices until after it came out following the robbery. If these things had been known, Ong said, Schreiber would have been dismissed from the bank.

So, where did the money come from that Schreiber spent so freely? Some thought that he had made some big money gambling in Indianapolis and Louisville. Local gamblers said they could never convince Schreiber to play their games, though.

It was later revealed that Schreiber had not just one fast horse, but a stable of them, which is how he was able to come into so much money. It was also later discovered that Fannie James, a very attractive woman, had come to Columbus from Chicago the day before the robbery, plied him with wine and persuaded him to commit the crime.

The day the robbery was discovered, the bank's president took off for Toronto, hoping to interview Schreiber and perhaps bring back some of the cash and the notes that had been stolen. Lucas, having no idea that Schreiber didn't head straight to Toronto after leaving Columbus, did not let the news of his plan leak out should Schreiber catch wind of it and go elsewhere.

Lucas took a train to Detroit, where he switched trains and headed for Toronto. As the train was about to roll into Toronto on Saturday morning, Lucas was sitting in his berth when the curtains in the berth on the other side of the aisle opened, and a familiar face stared at him.

"Hello there, Schreiber," Lucas said, recognizing his former employee, despite the fact that Schreiber had attempted to disguise himself by shaving his mustache and side beard off. His hair was also closely clipped and there was a "shining spot on the crown of his head a few inches across that had also been shaved, giving him the appearance, Lucas stated, of a Catholic priest." The change in appearance didn't fool Lucas.

Captain William J. Lucas, president of First National Bank, traveled to Canada to get some of the money back that Will Schreiber had stolen. *Bartholomew County Historical Society.*

A shocked Schreiber composed himself before returning the salutation.

The fact that Lucas and Schreiber ended up on the same train had shocked both of them. Schreiber had no idea Lucas was coming to Toronto. And Lucas thought Schreiber was already in that city. The night of the robbery, Schreiber traveled from Indianapolis to Chicago, where he got his new look. He then moved on to Milwaukee, where he deposited the securities and some of the cash in Merchants National Bank.

Schreiber took a steamer across Lake Michigan, then a sleeper car on a train bound for Toronto. It was that very same sleeper car that Lucas boarded at Detroit. One hundred miles later, the two met face to face.

The meeting was an uncomfortable one for both parties. They had known each other since Schreiber was an infant, and Lucas had thought Schreiber to be honest. Schreiber had occupied several positions of trust before ever taking a job at Lucas's bank. For a time, he had been thought of by many local residents as a model young man. But he had "turned out to be the prince of rascals."

When they arrived in Toronto, they went to the Queen's Hotel, where Schreiber, acting on Lucas's advice, registered under an assumed name.

That way, attorneys would not get ahold of the young man and try to secure fees from him or prevent him from signing an agreement with Lucas.

Lucas and Schreiber arranged an agreement in the hotel's parlor whereby $2,600 of the cash, as well as all of the securities that Schreiber had taken, would be returned. In exchange, Schreiber would be given immunity from prosecution as long as he never returned to the United States. If Schreiber hadn't agreed, Lucas would have had him arrested and extradited. The reason Lucas didn't try to make him pay all of the money back was that the rest of it would have been spent on attorneys' fees and other expenses anyway. By Monday, Lucas and Schreiber had moved on to Windsor, where the agreement was signed and made legal.

Despite giving back some of the money he'd stolen, Schreiber still had plenty left. He and James met in Canada and "engaged in licentious living on their ill-gotten gains." He purchased a schooner and lived a lordly life on the Great Lakes. He got careless sometimes, entering the United States from time to time. He almost got caught one night in Cleveland when he docked his boat there.

He and his companion decided thereafter to live solely on Canadian soil, settling in Toronto, engaging in the wholesale and retail tobacco business. He sold out of that and continued to live the life of luxury with James and then another woman.

Schreiber later told a reporter for the *Evening Republican* that the woman he ran off to Toronto with was actually named Jones and she had been a schoolmate of his when he was quite young. The two didn't stay together very long, as they often argued. Shortly thereafter, Schreiber said he met Ida Torrence, and the two of them stayed together until she most likely committed suicide in June 1890.

There is some confusion as to what exactly happened to Torrence. One account said she committed suicide by using Schreiber's revolver to shoot herself in the head in a hotel. But another said that Schreiber murdered her and spent much of his money trying to gain his freedom in Canada, which he eventually did. And yet another account said Torrence died of a morphine overdose.

Either way, after her death, Schreiber became bolder and was an easy mark. It wasn't long before Schreiber found another woman to spend his money on. This woman, who lived in Detroit, was said to have been induced by a detective to invite Schreiber to come to her place in late September 1890. When he arrived for the visit, she turned him over to the police.

With that, Will Schreiber was brought home to Columbus a seemingly broken and repentant man and placed in the county jail. After a few days, Schreiber decided that he would work out a settlement with the bank he had robbed, giving First National all the cash he had not spent, some stock and the deed to a property he owned in Montreal.

Those who visited him in jail said that Schreiber mentioned often how he planned to turn over a new leaf and placed all the blame for the crime upon himself. At this point, he was still only twenty-three years old.

"There is yet hope for Schreiber," a story in the *Evening Republican* stated. "But if his future is to become brighter as age grows on him it must all be brought about by his own commendable acts."

He pleaded guilty in court, and his attorney requested leniency in the sentencing. The bank he had robbed, meanwhile, had recouped all its losses, owing to Schreiber's deal. And even though First National officials felt it was their duty to have him tried in court, they felt no malice toward him and didn't wish for a harsh punishment.

Judge Nelson Keyes felt otherwise, however, sentencing Schreiber to twelve years in prison and fining him $500. The sentence was two years shy of the maximum the law allowed. For a man who had hoped to soon get his life on track in a positive way, Schreiber was extremely disappointed. As he was led from the courtroom, he became quite nervous and nearly broke down.

A reporter for the *Evening Republican* secured an interview with Schreiber just before he was to leave on a train bound for the Jeffersonville prison early the next morning. At 4:30 a.m., Sheriff William Smith opened the door of the north room of the Seventh Street station, and in walked Schreiber in irons, followed by the sheriff and deputy. Schreiber was smoking a fine cigar when he entered. He walked to the lunch counter, asked for a cup of coffee and a sandwich and sat down.

Judge Nelson Keyes sentenced Will Schreiber to twelve years in prison for robbing First National Bank in Columbus. *Bartholomew County Historical Society.*

He wasn't much in the mood to talk to a reporter. When informed that this would be his last chance for quite a while to speak to the people of Columbus regarding his crime, he said, "I leave this matter entirely in the hands of the bank officials. If they care to make a public statement of the condition of affairs they are at liberty to do so, so far as I am concerned, for it cannot injure me, and I have no desire to do them any further harm, but will say that the reports regarding the matter are in the main correct."

Schreiber did say he thought the sentence harsh "and greatly against my chances in the future. I thought Judge Keyes showed some signs of vindictiveness when rendering his decision, but I hold no malice against him on this account, for he is honorable and respected and must do his duty."

As the train whistle blew, signaling the time for him to board, Schreiber had a small request for the reporter. "Remember to not be too hard on me, for my mother lives here and this will trouble her."

James S. Brown, who was the judge when Schreiber was arrested, later tried to get First National Bank to give him a reward of $37,000 that he said was offered for the capture of the thief. But bank officials said that Brown hadn't had anything to do with the capture of Schreiber or the recovery of any of what was stolen. The court sided with the bank.

By all accounts, Schreiber was a near model prisoner. Less than three years into his sentence, he had become an assistant to the prison physician and surgeon, took great interest in his work, was industrious, read a lot and was told that if he kept up the good work, he would be a fine physician when he got out.

Will ended up not having to serve all of his sentence, as he was pardoned by Governor Claude Matthews just before Christmas 1894. Schreiber came home to visit immediately after his release but then left and apparently never returned.

A report surfaced in Columbus in October 1899 that Schreiber had been killed in the Klondike, but that was found to be untrue when he sent a telegram from Chicago verifying he was very much alive.

Five years later, another report came in that Schreiber was dead. This time, it appeared to be true. He had been playing cards on a Mississippi River riverboat sometime in late 1903 or early 1904. He reportedly grabbed the money off the table and jumped into the river. As he tried to swim ashore, the offended man stood on deck and shot him until he sank from sight. Schreiber's relatives confirmed the story but said no more about it.

In the end, Will Schreiber was never able to put his lust for money away for good, and it cost him his life.

8

BLIND TIGERS, BOOTLEGGERS AND BOOZE LAWS

When it has come to laws concerning the manufacture, sale and consumption of alcoholic beverages, Indiana has traditionally tended toward the dry side of the law.

During much of its history, state booze regulations have been some of the strictest in the nation. Indiana was totally dry for a few years in the 1850s and administered temperance vehicles such as "local option" and "blind tiger" laws.

Even today, it is one of less than a dozen states that prohibits the sale of alcoholic beverages on Sundays outside of restaurants, bars, microbreweries and artisan distilleries. The sale or serving of alcoholic beverages from 3:00 a.m. Christmas Day until 7:00 a.m. December 26 was banned until 2015. There is still a ban on Election Day alcohol sales while the polls are open.

Ever since the state's territorial days, Hoosiers have lived with limitations on the sale, manufacture and consumption of alcoholic beverages. Columbus and Bartholomew County certainly had their share of those who refused to obey whatever the booze laws were at the time, whether that meant running a backyard still, providing alcohol to minors, selling it at times other than allowed by law or without a license or simply consuming too much and behaving irresponsibly.

Even during times of legal liquor here, some skirted the law, and the saloons and taverns were bastions of filth, ne'er-do-wells and vice.

At one point, it was illegal to sell liquor to soldiers or Native Americans in the Northwest Territory, from which Indiana was carved. In the early

1800s, the territorial legislature banned the sale of liquor on Sundays or to minors.

During the mid-1800s, a prohibition tactic pushed by temperance groups called "local option" was popular. The law allowed counties to prohibit taverns and groceries from selling liquor if it was approved by majority vote. By 1847, the local option concept extended to nearly all counties. Statewide prohibition legislation was passed in 1855. But three years later, the law was ruled unconstitutional by the Indiana Supreme Court, and a license law was substituted for it.

From the 1890s through the 1920s, reformers interested in a "greater good" advocated such measures as women's suffrage, laws restricting child labor and the prohibition of making and consuming alcoholic beverages.

The Indiana arm of the Anti-Saloon League of America formed in 1898, and it worked with both political parties to achieve some of the driest legislation in the country. Indiana's legislature continued to pass increasingly restrictive prohibition laws. The blind tiger law, passed in 1907, allowed for the search and seizure of suspected illegal saloons. If convicted of operating a blind tiger, the defendant would receive a mandatory jail sentence, making this one of the strictest laws in the country.

Irish immigrant John Carr owned one of the vilest saloons in the city in the late 1800s and early 1900s. *Bartholomew County Historical Society.*

John Carr operated his saloon on Third Street between Washington and Jackson Streets during many of these changes in local booze laws. He ran what local historian William E. Marsh called the vilest of the dozen or so "plain hell-holes" in Columbus in the late nineteenth century. Carr's saloon sold "the biggest one in town for a nickel," and according to Marsh, Carr would not refuse a drink to any man, no matter his level of intoxication.

A native of Ireland who came to America in his teens and settled in Columbus in the 1860s, Carr was said to be quite a genial man. He rarely missed services at the Catholic church and served on the city council in the late 1880s and early '90s.

However, his saloon, later the site of the Wagon Wheel bar, was famous for its "white whiskey." And Carr got into trouble on more than one occasion due to events in and around his place.

He obtained his license to sell liquor in Columbus in 1879. Four years later, he was charged with selling liquor to minors but was acquitted.

Carr was later charged with illegally selling and giving away intoxicating beverages, as well as assault and battery. His defense didn't deny the charges but said that the arrest should have been made immediately instead of a half hour after the act took place. The law didn't agree and found him guilty on all counts.

He was also charged with selling on Sunday and violating the eleven o'clock law, which forbade the selling of alcohol between eleven o'clock in the morning and five in the afternoon on a national holiday, the Fourth of July, in 1885.

Carr was once again accused of selling liquor on the Fourth of July two years later. Marshal Pat Hagerty closed down three saloons that day that were not supposed to be open. Despite that action, some persisted in selling, and bartenders from Carr's and Palmer's saloons were arrested. Carr was acquitted on three of the four charges against him.

Palmer's bartender, Frank Spurgeon, meanwhile, was convicted. Spurgeon was accused of giving Billie Sharp a beer. Sharp testified that he went to the cooler and drew the beer himself, and Spurgeon neither gave the beer to him nor sold it. That argument didn't fly with the judge, who said that as long as Spurgeon was behind the bar, he was in control of who drank there or not.

The *Evening Republican* was happy to see someone get punished for breaking the booze laws, as it didn't seem to happen often during that time. "This should be an example to other saloon men in the city daily who violate the law, and the officials should see to it that every man who violates the liquor law receives his proper punishment."

There were benches in front of Carr's saloon that for years were used by men to wile away the hours, whittling, talking and waiting for a friend to invite them inside for a drink. Those benches were removed by the city in

John Carr's saloon eventually became the Wagon Wheel, one of the bars on Third Street across from the county courthouse that was demolished to make room for The Commons. *Courtesy of the* Republic.

1911, as officials seemed to get tired of too many "men of leisure" hanging around outside the saloon.

On one of those rare times when a patron was actually kicked out of John Carr's saloon, the man sued Carr for $5,000 when he sustained a broken leg upon getting tossed. Elijah Hankins alleged that in August 1913, he was wrongfully sold whiskey at the saloon, as he was intoxicated. Hankins said he was already staggering out of the bar on his own after the bartender, Robert Erskine, ordered him to leave, when Erskine unnecessarily pushed him out of the place, causing him to fall on the steps and break his leg. This, he said, made him a cripple for life.

It took two hotly contested trials (the jurors did not agree after the first one) before $250 was awarded to Hankins's wife, Zula, due to the loss of her husband's earning power.

Some might say that Elijah Hankins put up quite a stink at the second trial. At one point, Hankins was asked to remove his shoes and socks to show the jury both his healthy leg and his injured one. He stood on top of the table where his attorney, William J. Beck, had been sitting, to give the jury a good look. Beck at once sniffed the air, raised his eyebrows and moved back from the table with disgust. It became apparent that Beck felt as though Hankins had not washed his feet in some time. Beck refused to sit at the table again until it was washed of the dust that had fallen from Hankins's feet and was disinfected.

At least one good thing did come out of John Carr's saloon, though. A chimney sweep cleaning the chimneys there in July 1888 entertained anyone who could hear by singing some humorous songs.

If Carr ran one of the vilest saloons in town, Sam Sowers ran perhaps the most law-defying one. Sowers moved to Columbus in 1898 with an interest in purchasing the Klondike Saloon on south Jackson Street. After getting the Klondike, Sowers engaged in a litany of illegal acts.

He pleaded guilty to running a house of ill fame and evil association in 1900, stating that he would leave the city when his liquor license expired the following day. He reneged on that promise and was continually in court fighting various liquor law charges before selling the place in 1901.

Sowers later opened a saloon in his own name near Fifth and Washington. One night, Tob Evans, Sowers's nephew, who served as a bartender, awoke some folks who had been invited to take a nap upstairs. One of the men didn't like being aroused before he had finished his nap, so Evans fired his revolver a few times and scared everyone off, including the patrons downstairs.

Sowers was often accused of either selling alcohol to minors or allowing them to loiter in his saloon, neither of which were legal. Once he showed up in court to face nine separate charges. In July 1902, he pleaded guilty to assault and battery and was told to close his saloon and move out of Columbus. He was still in town in October and rearrested.

Sowers eventually promised to sell only soda if he was allowed to keep his saloon open. But city officials closed him up for good in August 1903, when his liquor license expired. Sowers, who then moved to Indianapolis, got nabbed for violations of the booze laws there, too.

Among the ploys that were tried here when local option ramped up and Prohibition seemed to be on the horizon was the quart shop. This was a place where people could buy prepackaged liquor and take it with them; one could not consume it in the shop. Robert Wilson ran the most famous quart shop in Columbus in the late 1800s: the First and Last Chance, at Fourteenth and California. But instead of sending his customers home with their purchases, Wilson provided a stockade in his backyard, where they could drink. The yard at Wilson's place got to be quite a mess after certain drinkers had their fill. And the owner wasn't afraid to break a few laws along the way.

A bloody fight between two customers in March 1897 seemed to be the last straw, and neighbors lodged several complaints against Wilson and his shop. After he gave up the quart shop, Wilson operated a few saloons in town, principally the Ping Pong on south Washington Street.

Moonshiners weren't the only ones to benefit from illegal liquor. In February 1911, George Golden, a prosperous farmer at Nortonburg, northeast of Columbus, said he was benefiting by the local option law that had turned the county dry a year earlier. With all the illegal drinking that was going on, people were throwing their beer bottles out on their way home on the highway near his farm, providing him with about one hundred empty bottles for his wife to put homemade ketchup in.

The term *blind tiger* was coined in the late 1800s to describe illicit drinking establishments that opened their doors as temperance legislation swept across the country. Such establishments, which sometimes also allowed other forms of illegal entertainment, were called speakeasies or blind pigs in other parts of the country.

Blind tigers were common in the early twentieth century here. And starting in 1908, many raids on them were conducted in Bartholomew County.

That fall, Columbus police raided a barbershop on Seventh Street owned by John Adams. In the rear of the shop, there were rooms attached where liquor was sold illegally. Six men were arrested. Police found a gallon and a half of whiskey and several beer bottles, some of which seemed to have been

THE POOR BLIND TIGER.

The legislature is showing a disposition to put him out of business.

Louis Richards's editorial cartoon suggests that the blind tiger was an endangered species in February 1907. *Courtesy of the* Republic.

recently emptied, in a back room. Implements of gambling were also found, but the men were not in the process of gambling at the time.

Adams was acquitted of the gambling charge. But he pleaded guilty to operating a blind tiger, even though he had stated earlier that he wasn't guilty. It might not be a coincidence that his confession came shortly after his wife wrote him, stating she was sick of living in Birmingham, Alabama, and wished to join him in Columbus as soon as possible. He was sentenced to thirty days in jail and fined. But he didn't have the money to pay the fine, and his stay was lengthened to eighty days.

While in jail, Adams contacted several of his sweethearts and tried to get them to pay his fine by appealing to their sympathetic sides. That didn't work. So he personally appealed to Judge Marshall Hacker and got out a few weeks early—only after promising to immediately go to his ailing wife, who was still in Birmingham.

It was not always easy for authorities to find blind tigers. In fact, sometimes it was darn near impossible.

In August 1909, a couple days after two suspected blind tigers were raided by Sheriff Irvin Cox, who failed to find any illegal activity, the *Evening Republican* summed up the difficulty officials had in catching the lawbreakers:

The sheriff of Bartholomew County and the police officers of the city of Columbus will have their hands full suppressing the illegal sales of liquor. Even now the air is full of rumors that liquor may be had for the asking (and the price) at numerous places where the law forbids the traffic....It will take a concerted effort to put into effect the law [prohibiting liquor sales in Bartholomew County] *which a large majority of those who voted in a special election favored. This ought to be ample backing for the officers to do a plain duty.*

The majority of the county, including the city of Columbus, had voted to try no saloons for two years. "They didn't want to try the experiment of blind tigers and bootlegging; they wanted to see what a community would be like where no liquor was sold," the newspaper said.

Officers knew who was selling liquor illegally, the story added, and that it was "up to them to bring down the heavy hand of the law."

In November 1909, the *Evening Republican* noted that while the county had voted itself dry several weeks before, the city of Columbus still was quite wet—illegally so. Some men, it was said, who had previously stopped in saloons to drink at every opportunity, had, in fact, started spending their time and money at home instead. However, drunkenness had not been stopped, and liquor was being sold in the city every day.

Drinking men, who could be spotted on the sidewalks of Columbus by their staggering walk and the odor of their breath, knew where to get liquor, although they were not letting on where those places were. More whiskey was reportedly being consumed illegally in dry Columbus than had been consumed legally in wet Columbus. One reason for that was many men who had drunk beer legally in saloons were now turning to illegal whiskey, as beer by the bottle had become difficult to obtain. Whiskey was easily had.

Whiskey was still legally available from druggists to treat certain ailments or used for mechanical or scientific purposes. One local druggist said he had nineteen requests for a quart of whiskey on a particular day; some of the men even brought prescriptions. But the druggist said he didn't sell to those men, as he knew they were just looking for a drink and not to use the beverage for medicinal purposes. Not all Columbus druggists operated that way.

Some of the druggists who refused to sell whiskey illegally lost business, as thirsty clients went elsewhere for the alcohol and stayed for other health supplies.

Owners of blind tigers sometimes found out ahead of time about a planned raid on their establishments and closed early. Sometimes, authorities were

COLUMBUS "DRY"
COLUMBUS "WET"

Look Into Local Conditions and Take Your Choice as a Result.

LIQUOR IS BEING SOLD

A newspaper headline in 1909 laments the fact that while no alcohol was supposed to be sold in Columbus due to the laws of the day, many men were still getting their fill of illegal booze here. *Courtesy of the* Republic.

fed bogus information. On one particular night in November 1909, three places in the city were raided, to no avail.

Near the end of 1909, Sheriff Cox offered twenty-five dollars to anyone who would supply him with information that led to an arrest and conviction in a blind tiger case. Cox said that he had searched several places he was sure

The blind tiger is a very hard animal to capture.

Sometimes, government officials were accused of looking the other way when it came to raiding blind tigers. *Courtesy of the* Republic.

were blind tigers, but that when he went, there was no booze to be found. He insisted that the owners of these establishments couldn't have been tipped off.

The way some of these blind tiger operators worked was that the owner would keep a small bottle of whiskey in his pocket. When a man came in looking for a drink, the proprietor supplied it from the bottle. When officers arrived, the proprietor stated that the bottle was for his own personal use. Nobody who bought the whiskey would testify against the owner. The only route officers could go was to have enough stool pigeons buy drinks and agree to say where they got it. That rarely worked.

"I want to see some of these places cleaned out," Cox said. "The officers get roasted all the time because they do not get the blind tigers and I don't believe there are any real blind tigers here where you can go and find a stock of liquor on hand."

Cox blamed the drugstores for a good portion of the drunkenness in town. He said that a man could buy a quart of whiskey at a drugstore, perhaps even legally. But then he would sell drinks from the bottle to other men.

Just eighteen hours after one of the times Columbus went completely dry, in October 1909, cigar maker Andrew J. Becht's house on south Jackson Street was raided on suspicion of illegal beer sales. Police found five cases of beer and some empty and partially empty bottles inside, as well as several men drinking beer from bottles. The trial ended in a hung jury when one member of the jury refused to vote guilty.

World War I gave progressives yet another reason to support Prohibition. Grain used to distill liquor or brew beer was needed to feed a war-ravaged Europe. In addition, many brewers were of German heritage, and with Germany now an enemy nation, it was easy to position alcohol consumption as an unpatriotic activity.

That may have been the final motivation needed to get the national Prohibition movement's goals achieved. On December 18, 1917, Congress overwhelmingly passed the Eighteenth Amendment, which prohibited the manufacture, sale and transportation of alcoholic beverages, as well as the import and export of such beverages. Two-thirds of the states needed to ratify it for the amendment to become law.

Indiana was the twenty-fifth state to ratify the amendment, and by mid-January 1919, the two-thirds majority was reached. Prohibition, known as the "noble experiment," officially began the following January.

Prohibition enforcement proved to be a challenge, and Indiana's legislature "found it necessary to plug some gaps" in national laws, according to *The Road to Prohibition in Indiana*. In 1921, state lawmakers made it illegal to possess alcohol or a still (the means of making alcohol) and banned the sale of products containing alcohol, such as hair tonics, that could be used for "beverage purposes." Indiana passed the nation's first drunken driver law in 1923 and enacted the Wright "bone dry" law in 1925, making a liquor buyer guilty along with the seller.

The appeal of liquor was too much for many to resist, even if it was illegal to make it, sell it, transport it and buy it. And Prohibition brought with it some unique events in Columbus and nearby areas.

Among the Ku Klux Klan's activities in the early 1920s here were helping authorities shut down illegal drinking houses. Local Klansmen did that twice within a month in 1923, helping with a booze raid at Roy Trenary's house at Seventh and Brown Streets in September and then helping bring in Ray "Dirty" Piercefield, who was known for making "white mule" whiskey on First Street. Piercefield was often brought in on public intoxication charges, too.

Another Piercefield, Harry, was known to sell illegal booze and have wild parties at his house east of the city. Officials raided his place in 1924, netting quite a haul: one hundred pints of bottled home brew, a ten-gallon jar of beer that was in the process of being brewed, a bottling outfit and other equipment.

Hazel McKinney was the first female in Bartholomew County to go to jail for violation of a booze law. The McKinney place, situated south of Columbus in an area known as Sweet Ireland, had a bad reputation when it came to illegal liquor. When it was raided in November 1925, Dillard Beatty was found in the basement near some liquor, and officers thought they heard liquid being poured out of a bottle as they descended into the area. Beatty was charged with illegal consumption and McKinney with maintaining a nuisance in violation of the liquor law.

After being convicted, but before she could serve her thirty days in jail, the twenty-six-year-old woman jumped a bond of $500. Relatives, who thought she might have gone to Indianapolis, tried to find her. She surrendered four days later and went to the women's prison in Indianapolis.

Columbus might have escaped much of the organized criminal activity associated with Prohibition, but that didn't mean some local residents didn't make some money delivering illegal liquor to the big cities. One local man, who only drove his car to church on Sunday, had no idea that his nephew was stealing the car during the week to run rum to Chicago.

As the Prohibition era went on, it was apparent that the law wasn't producing the positive effects its supporters thought it would; in fact, quite the opposite was true. In May 1929, the National Commission on Law Observance and Enforcement (popularly called the Wickersham Commission) reported that the per capita consumption of alcohol had increased 500 percent between 1921 and 1929, reversing a downward trend that had taken place between 1910 and 1920.

Normally law-abiding citizens trying to obtain alcohol helped support a new criminal class. Drinking became an unregulated, underground activity, and it was also very profitable. Without the expense of government excise taxes, profit margins were huge, and organized crime flourished.

Gangsters such as Al Capone raked in millions of dollars selling and transporting illegal alcohol. Capone reportedly earned $60 million untaxed per year violating Prohibition laws. Organized crime, in turn, fostered

Sheriff J. Walter Johns examines a homemade still found in a chicken house southeast of Columbus. Moonshining was big business in Columbus and surrounding areas, even into the 1960s. *Courtesy of the* Republic.

corruption, as wealthy and well-connected criminals had the means to bribe public officials to look the other way. Sometimes, entire city administrations, including police departments, were on the payroll of mobsters.

In addition, illegal booze led to unforeseen health risks. Bootleggers made alcohol with suspect ingredients, sometimes unwittingly producing a poisonous mixture.

The obvious shortcomings of Prohibition caused even some of its most ardent supporters, such as teetotaler John D. Rockefeller Jr., to change their minds and call for its repeal. Democratic presidential candidate Franklin Roosevelt promised that, if elected in 1932, he'd make sure to repeal it during his presidency.

In March 1932, Lawrence F. Orr, the state's chief examiner of the state board of accounts and a onetime Columbus resident, said that Prohibition was a loss of revenue for the government and increased crime. Many others saw the same thing, and by the next year, the law was repealed.

Even after Prohibition ended, illegal booze continued to be made here, and homemade stills were found up into the 1960s. But with so many legal establishments to sell products with ingredients the public could be certain of, the heyday of the blind tiger and its relatives had finally come to an end.

9

THE POISONING OF DR. GRIFFITH MARR

Dr. Griffith Marr had just finished assisting in morning surgery at Bartholomew County Hospital on Friday, February 4, 1977.

As was typical after such a morning, the veteran anesthesiologist went to the surgeons' lounge near the operating room to eat his lunch. His dish of fish and peas, covered by a metal lid bearing his name marked with tape, was sitting on an autoclave being kept warm, along with the dishes of other doctors that a cafeteria aide had taken to the room.

Marr noticed a white powdery substance on his peas, but didn't think much of it, believing it to be some sort of new seasoning the cafeteria had added. However, after two or three bites, he decided that the peas tasted unpleasant, with a strange metallic flavor.

Dr. Griffith Marr, pictured here in 1960, consumed poisoned food after assisting in surgery at Bartholomew County Hospital one morning in 1977. *Courtesy of the* Republic.

He immediately thought that the substance might be something harmful and ran to the washroom to induce vomiting. Despite that, he became ill and was not able to complete afternoon surgery. He soon became gravely ill and was hospitalized for forty-eight hours.

Analysis of the food revealed the presence of aconitine, a deadly poison not stocked at the hospital or used in medical practice. Also known as devil's helmet or monkshood, aconitine is found in the aconitum plant, which is extremely toxic, especially the roots and root tubers. People who ingest it can suffer from paresthesia and numbness of the face and limbs, muscle weakness in the limbs, hypotension, dizziness, confusion, chest pain, palpitations, ventricular fibrillation, nausea, vomiting, abdominal pain and diarrhea.

An *Indianapolis Star* story reported that when Marr noticed he'd been poisoned, he exclaimed, "Jake finally got me." "Jake" referred to E. Robert Jacobs, a staff surgeon at the hospital. However, when Marr, a husband and father of two, later made his deposition, he said he could not remember making such an accusation.

This was the second poisoning of a doctor at Bartholomew County Hospital within a few weeks. Dr. Larry G. Willhite, also an anesthesiologist and a member of the medical staff, suffered strange mood-changing sensations in the hospital that were suspected to come from ingesting a hallucinogenic drug placed in his food or drink.

And that time, too, a fellow doctor was implicated. Patricia Stillwell, then a surgical nurse at the hospital, said she purchased such a hallucinogenic drug, purple mescaline, from undisclosed sources at the request of Dr. Lindley Gammell. Stillwell said she gave the drug to Gammell. Another report stated that Stillwell and fellow nurse Pam Smith had put the mescaline on Willhite's food as a joke, though.

As the investigation into the poisonings, especially the Marr incident, proceeded, officials uncovered a tangled mess with bizarre tangents. Among the discoveries were a nasty rift among the surgical staff, threats made to officers, an alleged murder plot stemming from an affair between a nurse and doctor and a lawsuit filed for defamation of character.

All of these findings came to light after the Indiana State Police started investigating the Marr poisoning at the hospital's request. Almost two weeks after the poisoning, they met with hospital administrator Robert Borczon. In a story the next day, the *Republic* reported that a meeting had taken place regarding an attempt on a doctor's life, but the paper did not mention Marr by name nor that poison was the cause. Marr refused to answer a reporter's questions.

The facts that poison was the method and Marr the victim were revealed publicly on April 20 at a hospital board meeting, when a letter from Marr's personal doctor, Dr. Duane Sebahar, was read.

It was difficult for most anyone who knew Marr to understand why anyone would want to harm him. One letter to the editor published by the *Republic* said of Marr, "There is no doctor who has such integrity, professional ability, sincere caring for his patients and others around him."

Since the food was accessible by many people, a large number of current and former hospital employees were questioned and given polygraph tests. For more than a year, nothing of any substance came out of the probe.

In September 1978, nineteen months after the poisoning, Bartholomew County prosecutor Richard Donnelly said he had identified some suspects and had some evidence, but he didn't see an indictment likely in the near future. By this time, the state had taken its local officers off the case, which disappointed Donnelly.

"The state police have not followed through with it," he said. "I've gotten nothing but lip service from their superiors." The state police later resumed their investigation.

Finally, toward the end of 1978, due to information uncovered in the Marr case, officials made an indictment against Gammell. However, the indictment had nothing to do with Marr or any poisoning.

Officers discovered an alleged 1970–71 conspiracy between Gammell and Jean Girone, a surgical nurse, to murder her husband, Tony, an electrician at Reliance Electric Company at the time. The nurse and Gammell, who was also married, were reportedly having an affair. During that time, Girone, under psychiatric care for mental and emotional illness, attempted suicide twice. Jacobs, a close professional associate of Gammell, treated her on both occasions.

Girone told investigators that she and her husband moved to Murfreesboro, Tennessee, in 1973, two years after the alleged murder plot was conceived. She agreed to appear before a grand jury on the matter, but shortly before it was to convene, she was offered a five-figure sum of money to withhold information and testimony from the grand jury, she said. She was also threatened not to testify; she did not say by whom, but it was alleged that it was Gammell. He was later charged with witness tampering and attempted bribery.

The investigations into the Marr poisoning and Gammell cases proceeded simultaneously, with several of the same people involved in both stories. Those investigations centered squarely on the surgical department of Bartholomew County Hospital.

The front entrance of Bartholomew County Hospital as it appeared in 1977. *Bartholomew County Historical Society.*

Meanwhile, John Myers of the Columbus Police Department and W.R. Chandler of the state police, who had been investigating the cases, said they had been threatened with lawsuits and the loss of their jobs if they continued to pursue the poisoning case.

The officers said some people told them that they wanted to "burn them" and "see them fired." They quoted one threat as "we have presents for you," and one threat was presented to them as "sealed in blood."

"There has been and continues to be a strong effort to get these people off the case," said Donnelly, who added that he had endured significant pressure to drop the case.

The threats and pressure allegedly stemmed from things Myers and Chandler had said during the investigation. Donnelly supported both of the officers. "They've done an amazing job. They have overcome a lot of obstacles. There aren't too many officers who could have withstood the pressure."

Donnelly, Myers and Chandler never said who made the threats, but they said that they knew who it was, later implicating Jacobs.

When Myers gave his deposition, he said that he felt that Jacobs was threatening the investigation, although he alleged that he hadn't actually said that to anyone previously. The Columbus police officer explained that his opinion was based on information he had received from other people, as well as a tape recording of Jacobs's telephone conversations with Girone. Officers had given Girone a recorder to tape any conversation with Gammell, and she had also taped conversations she had with Jacobs on November 16 and 17, 1978.

In the first conversation, Jacobs referred to the officers as "scum" with "low IQs" and called them "the dirty of the dirties." He said he wanted to get them "reprimanded" and "straightened out." In the next day's talk with Girone, Jacobs reiterated that he was interested in getting the two policemen "straightened out" and having them "stop what they were doing." He threatened to "burn them." He concluded by saying that he wanted to serve Myers and Chandler a notice of a suit on Christmas Eve for a Christmas present.

Rumor and gossip abounded, and a number of the stories found their way into the media. One such story recounted a professional quarrel in the medical staff between a faction that included Jacobs and Gammell and another faction that counted Marr and Willhite among its membership. The rift concerned whether anesthesiologists should work full time at the hospital or if they should also be allowed to have outside practices. Jacobs and Gammell had outside practices, while Marr and Willhite did not.

Feelings ran strongly on both sides.

"It was really bad," recalled Sherry Howell, a surgical nurse at the hospital at the time.

Three of the four doctors who had leading roles in the two factions at the hospital had been fixtures in Columbus for more than two decades.

Both Gammell and Jacobs had come to the area to practice medicine in the mid-1950s. They both moved to Columbus in 1960 and were both in their mid- to late forties when Marr was poisoned.

Gammell was born in New York City and graduated from the Indiana University School of Medicine. He started his practice in Edinburgh in 1955 before moving to Columbus five years later, when he started his practice at 2756 Twenty-Fifth Street in Columbus and joined the county hospital staff, too.

Jacobs was a native of Kansas who graduated from the University of Kansas Medical School. He started practicing family medicine in Hope in 1957 and joined the staff at Bartholomew County Hospital at the same time.

He moved to Columbus three years later, opening a practice at 1919 Twenty-Fifth Street that he shared with Dr. Walter Able. Jacobs served the county as its coroner for several years in the 1960s. He completed his surgical training in 1969 and practiced general surgery until he retired.

At the time of his poisoning, Marr was fifty-eight, a lifelong resident of Bartholomew County and a sixth-generation descendant of pioneer families in the county. He graduated from the Indiana University School of Medicine and served in a medical unit in the U.S. Navy during World War II. He was the hospital's chief of staff for two terms and the county health officer in the 1950s.

Willhite was the youngster of the four. At about thirty years old, he was the relative newcomer, hired by the hospital in 1974. He was a graduate of the Indiana University Medical School and married.

Gammell continued to operate his medical practice while awaiting his trial, which was moved to neighboring Jennings County. Proceedings were postponed into 1980. But in April of that year, Girone said she would not testify on advice from her physician and attorney, giving medical reasons. That left officials with no evidence against Gammell, and the charges against him were dropped on May 20.

Dr. Lindley Gammell (*center*) is escorted to the Bartholomew County Law Enforcement Building on December 15, 1978, by Indiana state trooper W.R. Chandler (*right*). *Courtesy of the* Republic.

During the investigation into the Marr poisoning, rumors in town ran rampant. Some wondered aloud if some of the hospital's doctors were involved in drug trafficking. There was a rumor that the poisonings at the hospital were related to city police confiscating half an airplane load of marijuana at Columbus's Bakalar Municipal Airport. And some even thought that Marr might have poisoned himself to try to frame someone.

There was seemingly no end to the rumors and allegations that came out during this time.

Allegations from officers that Jacobs was either bisexual or had homosexual tendencies came out during interviews with Pamela Stillwell and Jean Girone. These statements were not part of taped interviews or formal statements made by them. And both suggested that the officers were the ones who made the allegations about Jacobs, either in statement or question form—they couldn't recall. The officers, however, said that in both cases, they were simply reporting what the women said when asked about Jacobs, who was married at the time.

Revelation of the rumors about Jacobs's sexual preferences was the main reason he cited in filing suit against the city and state later. Jacobs notified the city and the state in April 1979 that he was going to file a $1 million defamation suit against those entities, as well as both of their police departments. At that time, under Indiana law, anyone filing suit against a governmental agency had to give that agency 180 days' notice before legal proceedings could be filed with a court. Jacobs charged Myers and Chandler and Indiana State Police officer Richard Barker with making the defamatory statements.

At the same time Jacobs was notifying agencies of his intent to sue them for slander and libel, those agencies came to a standstill in their investigation into Marr's poisoning. The Gammell investigation had caused some complications and taken some manpower away from the Marr case, though prosecutor Joseph Koenig said the case was still open as of July 1981.

When Jacobs's suit was filed in January 1980, no monetary amount was listed. And besides the aforementioned targets of the suit, a couple of names were added: Columbus mayor Nancy Ann Brown, Indiana attorney general Theodore Sendak and Indiana State Police superintendent John T. Shettle.

Jacobs outlined his specific allegations when he filed pretrial documents with Johnson County Circuit Court, where the case had been moved. Saying that he "feels the burning brand as I observe people eyeing me," he alleged that city and state police referred to him as a homosexual and a bisexual; said he interfered with a police investigation; and implied that he sold drugs illegally out of his office. He denied all of these accusations, the documents said.

Jacobs also said that city police officials conspired with a police officer who faced disciplinary action to fabricate statements about Jacobs in exchange for the officer receiving $10,000 for his pension rights. He said that Myers and Columbus police officer Billie Keith Monroe, who was under threat of dismissal due to long-standing misconduct issues, cooked up a plan whereby Monroe would corroborate Myers's story that Jacobs was homosexual. Monroe would then get paid off, Jacobs alleged. In 1980, however, police officers were given the option to join a new pension program. Under the program, officers would be given $10,000 and not receive their pensions until they turned fifty-five. At that age, the pension benefits would rise at a much slower rate than under the old plan. According to court documents filed by attorneys for the Columbus Police Department, Monroe used the new program prior to resigning.

Jacobs also stated in court documents:

> At no time either before or after did I ever do or say anything regarding the Marr or Gammell investigations. Nor did I ever have any interest in them other than as a law abiding citizen favoring conviction of the guilty and acquittal of the innocent. But here defendants publicly imputed to me efforts to defeat justice and aid criminals [to] escape sanctions of the law.
>
> They withheld what they well knew, that I was active only in defense of my reputation. Instead of correcting the wrong they had done me they continued to try to intimidate me by inferring that I was implicated in an attempted murder, at least to being an accessory after the fact. This they did despite their knowledge that it was false as evidenced by Myers' deposition.

Because authorities suspected someone Jacobs knew and perhaps worked with as being Marr's attempted murderer, Jacobs said police accused him of knowing who did it, court documents said. Jacobs also stated that state police officer Barker said to Columbus Township trustee and former Bartholomew County Hospital director of security Roger Johnson, "We're going to take down Dr. Jacobs, too [along with Gammell] and a high rent lawyer with him. That plaintiff was dirty, and we are going to convict him, even though he is powerful. And when plaintiff gets arrested he will try to use medical records of his treatment of policemen for treatment for clap [gonorrhea] to force the chief of the Columbus Police Department to drop such charges. I know about his illegal activities."

E. Robert Jacobs looks over a book just after being named Bartholomew County health officer in 1978. *Courtesy of the* Republic.

Jacobs also charged Barker with telling former Bartholomew County sheriff Jimmie McKinney that Jacobs was dirty, would be indicted by a grand jury and go to jail and "it will be in all the papers." He also said that Barker told McKinney, "Oh, Jesus Christ, we are going to take Dr. Jacobs down. He is guilty of a felony and is selling drugs out of his office and he is going to jail."

Jacobs said his reputation had been sullied by the allegations over his sexuality, that it got out to neighboring counties and "even assault[ed] the tender ears of my daughter at Indiana University, Bloomington." All officers accused of wrongdoing by Jacobs said that any comments they made had been done so in connection with obtaining information for a criminal investigation.

Jacobs later announced he was suing the city for $2.55 million, and a trial was set for December 9, 1982.

But in August of that year, Judge Larry McKinney dropped three of the five counts in the suit, the ones dealing with comments made about Jacobs's sexuality. The judge cited a 1981 Indiana Supreme Court ruling that a police officer is protected from being sued as long as his conduct "is not so outrageous as to put it outside the scope of his employment."

The judge also stated that allegations that Myers and Chandler said they thought Jacobs might be guilty of attempted murder or assisting an attempted murder "cannot be construed in the manner" that Jacobs alleged. So, that count was dropped, too.

Both Myers and Chandler expressed relief at the news.

"Thank God. I'm glad it's over," Myers said to the *Republic*. "You'll never know what my family and I have been through."

Chandler said, "I just want to keep everything calm right now."

After that, all that remained of the suit was Barker's statements to the sheriff. And it wasn't long before Judge McKinney dropped that count, too.

Jacobs appealed, but that was denied by the Indiana Court of Appeals in October 1983. The court's ruling stated, in part, "Faced with an Agatha Christie–type factual mélange, the officers entered upon the investigation of the Marr poisoning, a criminal act, as was their duty as police officers." It went on to say that the officers conducted a routine investigation, "which included interrogating, checking, verifying, assessing and discarding information obtained from various sources, including rumor, gossip and endless minutiae."

The appeals court ruling said that police officers must be allowed to do their duty without fear of retaliation. Such investigations might not be conducted if officers risked personal ruin by the form of each question asked of a hostile witness.

And as for the comments made that Jacobs could have had something to do with the Marr poisoning, the court stated, "It requires a tortured construction to glean a meaning from the statements that Jacobs was guilty of attempted murder or assisting attempted murder."

Once again, Jacobs appealed, this time to the Indiana Supreme Court. But the high court said in April 1984 that it would refuse to hear the case.

Thus ended the last lingering case stemming from the Marr poisoning. The four doctors who played the biggest roles in the case all continued to practice medicine until they retired.

Willhite and his wife moved to Evansville in 1979, in the midst of the Marr investigation. He now lives in Colorado.

Jacobs retired in 2006 and died eight years later at the age of eighty-three. Gammell closed his office in 1995, moving to Tulsa, Oklahoma, the following year, after the death of his wife, Katherine. He died in 2006 at the age of seventy-nine.

Marr was quite active in the Bartholomew County Historical Society after his retirement. He passed away in 2002 from injuries he received in a fall at his home. He was eighty-three.

In the end, despite a lawsuit, charges of tampering and bribery and all sorts of other allegations, nobody ever served any prison time over any of the allegations that were raised. The matter simply faded into memory.

BIBLIOGRAPHY

Bartholomew County Steps Through Time. Columbus, IN: The Republic, 2007.

Columbus 125 Years. Columbus, IN: The Republic, 2007.

Descriptive Atlas of Bartholomew County, Indiana. Chicago: Acme Publishing Company, 1900.

Evening Republican, various issues, 1872–1966.

Hedeen, Jane. *The Road to Prohibition in Indiana.* Indianapolis: Indiana Historical Society, 2011.

History of Bartholomew County, Indiana. Chicago: Brant & Fuller, 1888.

Illustrated Historical Atlas of Bartholomew County, Indiana: Chicago: J.H. Beers & Company, 1879.

Indiana Journalism Hall of Fame website. "Members." Last modified 2016. http://mediaschool.indiana.edu/ijhf/2011-members.

Jacobs v. City of Columbus. Indiana Court of Appeals Decisions, 1983.

Marsh, William. *I Discover Columbus*. Columbus, IN: Semco Color Press, 1956.

Marshall, Robert J., Mildred Murray and Ross Crump. *History of Bartholomew County Indiana 1888*, Vol. 1. Columbus, IN: Bartholomew County Historical Society, 1976.

Moore, Leonard J. *Citizen Klansmen: The Ku Klux Klan in Indiana, 1921–1928*. Chapel Hill: University of North Carolina Press, 1991

National Center for Biotechnology Information website. "Aconite Poisoning." Last modified April 2009. www.ncbi.nlm.nih.gov/pubmed/19514874.

The Republic, various issues, 1967–2016.

Souvenir and Official Program: 19th Annual Encampment, Grand Army of the Republic, Department of Indiana and Auxiliary Societies, Columbus, IN., May 17–20, 1898. Louisville, KY: Courier-Journal Job Printing, 1898.

ABOUT THE AUTHOR

*P*aul J. Hoffman likes to find the facts of the matter. He enjoys discovering the answers to questions. He's honed his abilities in that area throughout his thirty-year career as a journalist, and he's done it with his two published books.

A Wisconsin native and graduate of the University of Wisconsin–Milwaukee, Hoffman started his journalism career as a sportswriter for the *Milwaukee Sentinel*. He has also covered sports

Photo by Art Mellor.

for Pioneer Press newspapers in the Chicago suburbs and the *Shelbyville (IN) News*. He has served as the special publications editor at the *Daily Journal* in Franklin, Indiana, since 2001.

A resident of Columbus, Indiana, Hoffman's first book, *Murder in Wauwatosa: The Mysterious Death of Buddy Schumacher*, was published by The History Press in 2012.

He is the author of hundreds of articles and columns published in newspapers and magazines and is a member of the Bartholomew County Historical Society.

Hoffman is married and has four children, two stepchildren and one granddaughter.

He can be reached by email at phof63@sbcglobal.net, via mail at PO Box 2611, Columbus, IN 47202 or at his website: PaulHoffmanAuthor.com.

Visit us at
www.historypress.net
....
This title is also available as an e-book

CPSIA information can be obtained
at www.ICGtesting.com
Printed in the USA
LVHW070825251121
704228LV00030B/2653